MW01602533

OG WILLIE J

The Jack of All Trades

MINISTER WILLIE WIGGINS JR AKA
REVEREND OG WILLIE J

PublishAmerica
Baltimore

Hardcover 978-1-4560-8006-8
Softcover 978-1-4560-6835-6
PUBLISHED BY PUBLISHAMERICA, LLLP
www.publishamerica.com
Baltimore

Printed in the United States of America

INTRODUCTION

I am now 52 years of age and I have had the pleasure of holding many occupations in life. Some good and some bad, but all have given me the experience in life to be the man that I am today.

I have experienced, and indulged in almost every type of con and hustle that there is, and I became good at them. I have mingled with the stars (sports & entertainers alike). I entertained the good, the bad, the beautiful and the ugly.

I earned over a million dollars at a very young age, and has witnessed things that would make a Billy goat puke! I am not only street wise but also educated, having degrees in Psychotherapy, Accounting, Business Administration, Marketing, Ministry, EMT, and Computer Business Specialist.

I would not trade these experiences for nothing in this world because I know that the experience is the best teacher. This story of the many occupations that I have held in my life tells of the many journeys, Adventure, experiences, opportunities, trails & tribulations, violence, money, women, and drugs that I was involved with at different stages of my life.

This book will bring you on an emotional rollercoaster ride that will have you laughing, crying, sad and angry. I have had many opportunities for success in my life, but Satan had got a strong hold on me at an early age. This book will tell you how one man could endure so much hardship, pain, torture, hate and tragedy and come out a champion!

Also to have so much love, be tenderhearted, caring, forgiving, thoughtful, and charitable with so much positive energy that it would have balanced out the universe.It has been said that the truth hurts; and that the truth will set you free.

Let me introduce Willie Wiggins Jr aka Og Willie J:

While writing this book I found that the truth has hurt and has set me free also. While I share my life's experiences, the trials and tribulations of this true story will shock many people. I pray that none of you ever go through what I've been through in life because not everyone will come out of this the way I was blessed to come out of it.

While I know that GOD exist and I know of HIS infinite power, I know that GOD allows us to make our own choices in life which will decide our fate. this in turn makes you and I the master of our fate. I have experienced both positive and negative aspects of life.

Many doors have opened for me creating many opportunities for success. As I now pray for the knowledge of GOD's will for me and the power to carry it out, I have never waited for GOD's answers until now.

It is a good thing to have the freedom to make our own choices in life but remember, when we make choices, we set in motion a chain reaction of either positive or negative things or events to happen in our lives. We all have to live with the choices that we make in life. So before you make a decision in life, think about it. It's your choice and your fate. Which way will you choose?

4

TABLE OF CONTENTS

OCCUPATIONS HELD BY WILLIE J

POSITIVE JOBS	NEGATIVE JOBS

POSITIVE JOBS	NEGATIVE JOBS
1. Shoe shine boy	34. Gambler
2. Newspaper boy	35. Drug Dealer
3. Ice Cream boy	36. Pimp
4. Short order cook	37. Thief
5. Gas station attendant	38. Con Artist
6. Asst. Restaurant manager	39. Gigolo
7. Accounts payable Clerk	40. Escort Service manager
8. Restaurant general manager	41. Thug
9. Accounts receivable Clerk	
10. Office manager	
11. Liquor store clerk	
12. Armed security guard	
13. Insurance salesman	
14. Carpet cleaner	
15. Motivational Speaker	
16. Construction	
17. Roofer	
18. Landscaper	
19. Maintenance supervisor	
20. Fashion Model	
21. Actor	
22. Musician/singer	
23. Performer/Entertainer	
24. Music producer	

25. Entertainment manager
26. Concert promoter
27. Boxer/prize fighter
28. Emergency Medical Technician
29. Staff accountant
30. Substance abuse councilor
31. Minister/Pastor
32. Soldier in the Army
33. Retail manager

PREFACE

Some people would say that it is better to be a master of one trade then it is to be a Jack of all trades. I say that the experienced is the best teacher and that it is great to have many skills. My life has been an emotional roller coaster ride, never stable and never consistently on the right or wrong path of life.

I know that you can't serve two masters, (GOD & Satan) at the same time and do it Successfully, even though I tried to at times. I worked 45 occupations in my life both positive and negative, but the negative jobs were lengthy and out weighted the good for most of my life, until now!

This book is the true story of my life and will take you on an emotional rollercoaster ride with will shake the very ground that you walk on.As you read this book don't allow yourself to be drawn to the negative lifestyles that sounds so glorious, adventurous and prosperous.

It is only temporary and leads to jails, institutions and death. Pick a profession or trade that you love and enjoy doing and master it. Hone your skills and stick with it that you may enjoy the fruits of your labor.

FOREWORD

This book is not intended to glorify my life or any part of it. It is not intended to belittle or downplay any of my love ones, friends or family. With the exception of few, everyone that is mentioned in this book has matured, changed their way of life, and thinking.

Please don't judge anyone that I mention in this book for all have sinned and fall short of the glory of GOD! I want all that read this book to know that even though my mother and father were strict and I don't agree with the method's they used to discipline me, my brothers and sisters,

I know that they loved us and did what they thought was right. The real culprit in this book is me! I was a very viscous, evil and wicked man and I had to mature, repent, and make adjustments in my life. So for all of those who are offended by me, please forgive me as I tell my life story in this book. Og Willie J The Jack Of All Trades!

DEDICATION

First and foremost, I would like to dedicate this book to the father (GOD), the son (Jesus Christ), and the Holy Spirit, for allowing me to experience everything that I have experienced in my life. My parents Martha and Willie Wiggins Sr in which through love and GOD brought me into this world and provided for me. I thank you for the adjustments that you have made in life to show your love & attention to our family & be the great parents that you are; I honor you mom and dad!

Theresa Wiggins you are making great strides & adjustment in life, God bless you and I love you dearly! My Children Willie #1, Willie #2, Tanika, & Eunice, Wiggins, and my grandson Jaden Wiggins, I love you all dearly as I share my life's experiences and offer my personal assistance and guidance in your lives. Peace and blessings to my brothers and sisters I love you all dearly;

Pamela, Marcus, Khyam, Mibsam, Almetra, Lydia, Ella, Ariel, Karima, and Eleka Wiggins. My cousin Serena Grooms who's Godly spirit I admire and love! All of my aunts, uncles, nieces, nephews and cousins who are too many to name but I love you all. My deceased loved ones

R.I.P, (Nana) Carrie Sweeney, Mayo, (Grandma) Lillian Mckinney, My sisters Miranda, Nadina, and Shemida Wiggins. Nephew Michael Wiggins, Uncle Ricky and Aunt Sister Mckinney, cousin Kevin Stokes, Big Mike, Teddy Tismo D Faulk, and Marvin Jones. To all that reads this book GOD BLESS YOU!

13

Strongroots_prod@yahoo.com
williewigginsjr@aol.com
Call Strong Roots Productions for bookings of Willie J: 941-623-7897

CHAPTER 1

In the Beginning

As far back as I can remember, I never remember my parents telling me that they loved me as a child. Even though I now know that they loved me, they didn't express it with hugs and kisses and by telling me. In fact I'm the only sibling that doesn't even have a baby picture even though I was the first born son.

I grew up in a family of four brothers and nine sisters, in a very close family. My parents were American Muslims who followed under the leadership of the not so Honorable Elijah Muhammad, and they were very strict, and the first school that I went to was a Muslim school.

My father opened a restaurant which was successful and was a good provider though. As a child at the age of 10 they taught me that Caucasian people were the blue eyed devils and were graphed from the black race of people. I know it sounds funny but as a child I used to wonder about that because most of the white people that I knew had brown or black eyes, so I figured that they were not devils.

As a matter of fact the devil don't discriminate, he don't care what color you are, he just wants to possess you and destroy you anyway he can. I remember when the so called Honorable Elijah Muhammad was sick and dying and I told one of the Muslim school teachers that I heard that he was dying on the

15

radio news show that morning, the teacher slapped me and told me that the Messenger (Elijah Muhammad) was GOD and would never die. I fought him back and he fell down the stairs and broke his arm. The next day the Messenger was pronounced dead.

We didn't celebrate Christmas because it was against the religion of the said nation of Islam.We celebrated what was called Saviors day on February 26th every year in which we exchanged gifts. But Christmas was always a sad time of my life because we never would have a Christmas tree and all of my friends would get a tree and toys. To this day I love sitting and staring at my Christmas tree and it is one of my favorite times of year now.

My first occupation came as a newspaper boy selling Muhammad speaks newspapers, and I was good at it. My father would send me and my brothers out with other Muslims of all ages and we would go to Huntington Ave in Boston Massachusetts and sell them to a majority of all white people.

They were our best customers and I would out sell everyone else there with me. All of my Muslim friends were older than me and we weren't allowed to go to movie theaters or birthday parties and would fast during the month of December, called Ramadan. This meant that we couldn't eat until the sun went down and then we could only eat fish and vegetables.

There wasn't much that I liked about being a Muslim because I felt that they were prejudice, too strict, and from what I had read about Islam, what they practiced was not a part of the Islamic religion but that of Elijah Muhammad's way.

I know that my parents loved me and were great providers of 14 children but they were very strict as Muslims under the leadership of Elijah Muhammad. They started beating me with belts, extension cords and broom sticks whenever I did anything that they didn't approve of. The more I became rebellious the more beatings I got, and the more intense the beatings became.

My uncle Ricky was a good friend and protector, and would always tell me that one day, we would run away together. Whenever I had fights or problems with other guys I would call Ricky to help me handle them. He was two years older than I was, and was quite a hustler.

I remember him making a shoe shine box and he would go downtown Boston to shine shoes to make money. He would always have $30.00 to $50.00 dollars whenever he came back from shining shoes so I asked him to show me how to make a shoe shine box and to teach me to shine shoes and he did.

I was 13 years of age at this time and I started going down town to shine shoes after school and would make $20.00 to $50.00 a day shining shoes. I saved $3,000.00 in a year time and I kept it underneath my mattress and one day it disappeared.

I never asked anyone who took that money but I always thought that my parents took it, and that made me very bitter and I wanted to get even so I started stealing money from my mother's pocket book and from my father's money box that he had in his bed room.

By this time my father had started making me come to his restaurant every day after school and taught me to be a short order cook. I had to work for him for five too six days out of the week for less money then I made shining shoes.

Now the beatings that I got from my parents continued and were getting more and more severe. I would get a beating for anything that I did that they didn't approve of, and I remember being scared of my father, so I would hide whenever he would come home.

I was still angry about my money being stolen because I worked hard for it by shining shoes, so I started stealing money from my parents every chance that I got. I started taking my father's silver coins from his money box in his bed room and would go outside and share with my friends.

I told them that I had found a treasure chest in the woods and one of my friends told his parents who told my parents. That's when my father found out and beat me with an extension cord.

I was standing in the doorway of my bedroom as he beat me so bad that blood was dripping from my groins. I told him that I needed to go to the hospital but he told me to go in my room and he slammed the door and walked away.

I deserved to get a butt whipping but not to that extent. Sometimes I did deserve to get my butt beat by my parents but I got some terrible butt whippings that I didn't deserve all the time also.

Once I reached over and took a pancake off the plate that had stacks of pancakes on it and my mother hit me on the head with something. I'm not sure but I think it was the frying pan. Another time I was arguing with my sister and my mother hit me on the back of the neck with a broom and broke the broom on my neck.

These are times that I remember that were over the edge butt whippings and caused me to be terrified by my parents. I don't believe in a blue print as to the correct way to discipline or raise your children but these are things that no one should do to their children. Show your children love and tell them you love them every day!

My father and my uncle Kimraf taught me how to play chess and I got so good at it within a month that I would beat everyone that I played, included my father and uncle. I even joined the chess team in school and would beat my chess teacher who was also the math teacher and he would be embarrassed that I beat him all the time in front of the class so he wouldn't play chess with play until after the class was over.

One night my father and uncle came home and my father called me to come and play chess with them. I played and beat them both each and every game that we had played. They then teamed up together and I still beat them.

It was late and I told my father that I was tire and wanted to go to bed but he slapped me in the face and told me to make my move. I was so tired that I purposely let my father, and my uncle who had teamed up with my father, beat me in that game just so that I can go to bed.

After the Muslim school closed down my parents put me into a school called the Highland park free school, which was another private school. It was predominately black and I was smarter than most of the other children.

I remember coming home after taking a test and telling my father that I got a B on my math test and he slapped me in the face and said "next time get an A". Like I said, my parents were very strict but excellent providers.

They took us on trips to other states and brought me and all of my 13 brothers and sisters bicycles and clothes to wear. They provided us with food, clothing and shelter.

It was at the Highland Park Free School that I started having a real interest in girls but the boys would pick on me all the time. I didn't know how to fight so I would get my ass kicked by every boy who attacked me and I would run home.

One day I was running home and my mother and father were home and saw me run up to the porch. They met me at the door and my father told me to get out there and fight or he would beat my butt.

I did go to fight and I actually got off some punched but still got my ass whipped. The next day my father took me into the back yard and started teaching me how to fight.

I would get blamed at school by the other kids whenever something would happen and even when I knew who did something wrong I kept my mouth shut, and took the blame for it and when I got home I got my ass whipped.

I got my first girlfriend at the Highland Park Free School. Her name was Gloria and all the guys wanted to be her boyfriend. But because she was my sister Nadine's best friend, Gloria became my girlfriend. I got a lot of girlfriends through contact with my sisters.

As a matter of fact I dated most of my sisters friends at one time or another. I was fourteen years of age and was on my way to meet Gloria at the school yard, and a woman that lived down the street from me named Serena was bringing in some groceries, and asked me if I would help her and I did.

She asked me if I wanted something to drink and I said yes and she asked me to sit down. She then gave me a magazine and asked me to read it while she went into her bed room. She left the door open so I could see her and she took off her clothes.

The magazine was a penthouse magazine and while I was looking at it the light bulb blew out and it went dark in the living room. She asked me to help her change the light bulb and she got a chair to stand on.

She got up on the chair and asked me to hold her legs. She had a see through night gown on with nothing else on underneath it and threw the night gown over my head. She asked me to help her down and then she grabbed me and started kissing me, putting her tongue in my mouth.

That was the first time that I experienced a French kiss. I was a virgin at that time but I guess by nature you automatically know what to do because I went to work having sex with her and she enjoyed every minute of it.

This went on for quite some time, two to three times a week and for two to three hours a day. I told my friend Harvey about it and he told my girlfriend Gloria and it broke her heart, and she didn't want to see me anymore.

Harvey then went to the woman Serena who I was having sex with, and asked her if he could help her with anything around the house, and she let him in and had sex with him. I never went back to see her. She tried to call me upstairs to her apartment several times but I ignored her each time.

All of my friends were two to three years older than me and couldn't believe it when I told them about this, because they all knew that she was a beautiful woman, a school teacher and they wanted her.

I was a really good basketball player also and I had a friend named Gorge that was very popular and good as me in basketball. We would go all over Roxbury and Dorchester to other basketball courts and challenge other ball players to a two on two game against us.

21

MINISTER WILLIE WIGGINS JR AKA REVEREND OG WILLIE J

We would play them for a $20.00 to $25.00 a game. We would play six to ten games a day a on Friday's and Saturday's, and have $100.00 by the end of the day. One day at the basketball court I was telling a guy named Gregory who was 20 years of age about Serena the woman who had seduced me, and he asked me if I wanted to hang out with him. I did and we went to the Highland Park Free School youth center to shoot some pool, but when we got there it was closed.

He said to me, let's break in and get the money that they have there because he stated that he knew where the money was. He also said that they had just got some new Polaroid camera's, which were the happening trend for cameras at that time. So we broke into the youth center and made our way upstairs.

He pulled a knife out on me and demanded that I take off my pants. I looked at him and said what are you doing man and he put the knife up to my neck and tried to unzip my pants. I shoved him off me and backed up, and ran under the pool table and he ran after me. I ran down the stairs with him close behind me, and then I came to the door and there was a brick there that would hold open the door all the time.

I grabbed the brick just in time as he grabbed my shirt and I turned around and hit him in the face with the brick. I continued to hit him until he passed out and blood was dripping from his head. I wanted to kill that booty bandit, and I damn sure tried but he survived.

Everyone in the neighborhood heard about what happened to him but until now no one knew that it was me that did it or even knew why it happened. I only told one person about what had happened at that time and that was my friend Harvey.

22

That faggot never came back around my neighborhood though, and I never seen or heard anything else about him. The Highland Park Free School closed down soon after that and I went to a public school.

At that time the public school system in Boston Massachusetts was busing Afro American students to all white schools in South Boston and Charlestown high schools. They were very prejudice, and the racism was among the worst in the country. I saw the white people throw bricks at the school buses as we pulled up to the schools and they attacked the black students with baseball bats, sticks, rocks, and knives.

The thing that was scary about that was that it was the parents standing along with their children (the Students), doing the attacking and they were trying to hurt us, or even kill us. I remember seeing one of the black football players shot to death on the foot ball field by a prejudice white man who didn't want him to play, and another foot ball player shot and became paralyzed.

I saw the American flag rammed up the nose of a black man who marched to the state capital build in protest of the racial violence. I was even kicked out of the public school system for fighting back the racist white students who taunted and attacked me, but nothing was done to them who attacked me and they were allowed to stay in the public school.

These things that happened I never talked about to anyone, not even my parents because I was afraid to. Parents I'm telling you to develop a interpersonal relationship with your children. A relationship of love and trust.

I was sent to another private high school called the experimental model high school in which I was the youngest student there, and I was given a double promotion. All of the other students were two and three years older then I and they all smoked cigarettes.

There was a girl that I liked and I wanted to fit in with them so I started smoking cigarettes also. I started on a Monday and everyday for that week I smoked and when the weekend came and I didn't have any cigarettes. I started craving for one and I went out knocking on my neighbors doors for a cigarette in which I told them that my mother wanted a cigarette.

They all knew that my mother didn't smoke and wouldn't give me one. I was craving so badly and became sick that weekend from not having one. It was the worst feeling I ever had. The sickness lasted for that weekend of three days and when it was over and I returned to school I never touched another cigarette in my life.

After school I would go to my father's restaurant to work a few hours and on weekends I would work there also. I was able to save up enough money, and brought a brand new car before I even got a drivers permit.

I started hanging out with my uncle Ricky and his gang of thugs and two of my friends, Calvin and Teddy. I was the one who had a car so they all wanted to hang out with me. We would go to parties all over the city.

Most of my friends smoked marijuana except me and my buddy Teddy. We thought that smoking marijuana was such a terrible thing to do and looked at it as a terrible drug. My uncle Ricky was a couple of years older than I was and was smooth with the girls. He taught me how to rap (talk) to girls, and manipulate them into having sex with me.

He also taught me how to gamble by playing craps and shoot pool in which I became good at. I was doing all of these things and as an American Muslim I wasn't supposed to be doing any of these things. I was very rebellious though. I was also very cunning.

One day me, my uncle Ricky, Calvin and a couple of other friends was on our way to a party. My friends was smoking weed in the car with all the windows rolled up, and I got a contact.

All of a sudden a drunken man ran his car into mine and smashed my car. It's amazing that none of us were hurt, but that night my father found out about what I was doing and whipped my butt and grounded me. He made me park the car in the garage and put me on a one month house arrest.

That's when I started sneaking out of the house to go to parties. I would wait until my parents went to bed or until they were in their bedroom with the door closed and then I would climb down the back porch or out of the basement window and go out to parties.

One day I came home at 3am and I climbed through the basement window and when I got to the top of the basement door, my father was standing there with the extension cord. He beat my ass again and I chilled out for a while.

My uncle Ricky was putting together a singing group and I wanted to be in it but he didn't let me be in it so I formed my own group. My sister Nadina also formed a singing group and we all entered a talent show contest in which my group won. My uncles group came in second place and my sister in third place.

The newspaper wrote an article about me and then my mother brought instruments for my 3 brothers and myself, in which they didn't want to learn to play them. I had experienced the attention that you get from performing and I loved it and I wanted more of it.

My mother saw how musically inclined I was, and enrolled me at the Warren Community School for music to help to keep me off of the streets. I learned how to read and write music and I loved it.

After music school I would go up into the attic of our house and practice playing these instruments, playing along with top 40 R&B music, unto I learned to play them effectively. I latter formed a band and started writing music for us to record on an album. CD's weren't even on the market yet.

One of my neighbors and friends was a group of brothers by the name of "The Johnson Brothers" which included the entertainers, and producers, Maurice Starr and his brother Michael Johnson. They was very poor but they had a recording studio in their house.

They were both order then I but they liked me because I was talented. I started writing love songs and party songs and recording the songs at their recording studio. I was on the path of becoming a great entertainer.

They had a home that was run down with no windows or heat in it and always wore the same clothes. Maurice Starr and I would play basket ball together and we were both good at it. All the guys at the basket ball court would make fun of him though, because he had run down sneakers and holes in his pants that he wore over and over.

I would never laugh at him though and he told me that one day he would make millions of dollars. He wrote some songs for me and wanted to put me into a singing group called the pretty boys.

I didn't like the name pretty boys and I also thought the songs that he wrote for us were too young for us, "Candy Girl" and "Popcorn Love". After I refused to sang those songs I started recording under the direction of Maurice's brother Michael Johnson, and Maurice never wanted to work with me again.

He produced the New Edition group and the New Kids on the block and they all went on to became two of the biggest singing groups in show business. My father didn't like me being into music, and would criticize me saying music is for faggots, and we would argue about that.

Never the less, I continued to entertain and still to this day I am still writing and producing music, (LOOK FOR MY GOSPEL CD IN STORES the year 2012).

Because of the physical and verbal abuse and torment that I was experiencing at home I ran away from home with my uncle Ricky and I got an apartment with him. My father found out where we were staying and sent some Muslim brothers to rough me up and bring me back home.

My uncle Ricky and I kicked their asses though, and sent them back with black eyes and bloody noses.

Finding the right note

After many detours, musician Willie J. Wiggins is doing what he does best

BY CHRISTOPHER MUTHER
CONTRIBUTING WRITER

It's taken him 20 years to do it, but Tent City resident Willie Wiggins has overcome a checkered past, left a successful career as a drug rehabilitation counselor behind, and returned full-time to his first love — music.

Wiggins, who performs under the name Willie J, recently inked a publishing and distribution deal with a subsidiary of Warner Bros. Records called Timberland. According to Wiggins, Warner/Timberland will release the singer's soulful remake of Curtis Mayfield's "Give Me You I Love" as a four-song maxisingle on CD and cassette in early April. An album will follow this summer.

"This is what I've been working

> 'This is how I'm going to make a living... All I want to do is what's right in this world.'
> —Willie J. Wiggins

want through the whole thing of selling drugs I was in trouble with the cops all the time, the whole bit. No matter what was happening — I could be high as a kite, and I was still playing music. That has always been a part of my life."

In 1995, while he was working as a drug counselor, Wiggins put his

to support the act, Wiggins decided to leave his day job at the Framingham Detoxification Center last year and pursue music, his dream since he was a teenager.

"I've waited for a few years to be able to start my own label," he says. "This is my own label, it's a legitimate business. This is how I'm going to make a living. I'm not going to do anything more illegal. I don't have to, and I've worked hard to get in that point."

Growing up on Northampton Street, Wiggins says, he was always musically inclined. When he was 12, his uncle bought him a harmonica that he carried with him day and night, until his parents bought an attic full of instruments for him and his four brothers.

29

CHAPTER 2

Coming of Age

I continued going to school and I graduated from a private high school called the Roxbury Medical Technical Institute. That is where I met my high school sweetheart Sharon. She was a shy girl and had a quiet and gentle spirit and she helped me to stay focused on education because she was a very smart girl. She also helped to keep me from wanting to party so much.

She was my first love, and the love of my life, and we did everything together, and went everywhere together. She experienced smoking her first marijuana joint with me and a couple of years later sniffing we sniffed our first line of cocaine with together.

We had sex every chance that we got, and there was nothing that I wouldn't do for her. I just thought the world of her and no one was ever going to come between us. We was a great couple until I started smoking weed regularly and occasionally sniffing cocaine.

After high school she went to Boston University and I went to Newbury College, and majored in accounting because my father wanted me to do that. I got my associates degree in accounting and I went to work for a company called Kendal Company as an accounts payable clerk. I also worked for my father's restaurant during the weekend.

Sharon moved into an apartment with me and two other girls and I also went back to work as a manager of my father's restaurant. My father was still very strict and mean, and even though he wouldn't hit me anymore he would still embarrass me by calling me names and threatening me in front of my friends and girlfriend.

He soon opened up another restaurant and leased it out to me for $350.00 a day. I became very popular and the restaurant was doing very well, but I was very young and so smart that I out smarted my own self. I had my own restaurant and I became buck wild.

I was partying and doing cheating on the love of my life Sharon but she had no idea that I was doing the things that I was doing. I did continued to write songs, practicing music, and also was going to the gym training.

I loved boxing and I was good at it in which you'll read about in a later chapter of this book. As I said I became very popular and started partying a lot, smoking marijuana, drinking and sniffing cocaine on the weekends.

I was a very handsome man, and women were very attracted to me. They came onto me everywhere I went even Sharon's friends. Sharon was still the love of my life but I was letting all the attention from women go to my head. I started having sex with some of her friends as well as other young ladies.

I believe that Sharon may have found out about. I had hired her brother and sister to work at the restaurant and I told her brother about a girl that I meant and had sex with and he told her. She then knew that I was sleeping around because she broke off our relationship.

31

That was my first and last time experiencing a broken heart. She would come by to visit me from time to time and but one day I asked her to cook breakfast and she made me some eggs with lumpy grits.

At this time I was slipping into darkness because of my frequent drug use and my attitude had changed. I remember getting so angry that I yelled at her and she started crying and left out of my apartment. That was definitely the end of that relationship.

She was a great dancer and went on to do bigger and better things with her life. I'm glad that she did because I would have ruined her life! One year later she came into my restaurant and asked me if I would meet with a friend of hers by the name of Allan Hayden.

He was starting up a concert promotion company called Allan Hayden Productions and wanted me to invest $2000.00 with him to promote recording artist Roy Ayers at the Berkley Performance center in Boston.

I declined and several years later Allan Hayden was one of the biggest promoters in the country. He is now one of the biggest promoters in the world and a multi millionaire. The restaurant became very, very popular though with stars, both entertainers and athletes a-like coming to eat there every day.

I had it going on; Money, Women, a nice car, a home, and fine clothes. But my father still was the same mean ass man that he always was. I would come into the restaurant and he would still embarrass me by talking down at me, and calling me names.

Even though I was leasing the restaurant from him he wanted to control me and would brawl beat me, (verbal abuse).

32

One day he came into the restaurant and started calling me names and yelling at me. I was so fed up with his disrespect for me that I gave him the keys to the restaurant and told him to run it himself. I was through with it and walk out.

I decided that I was going to go to Las Vegas and then to California to become a star. You see, by working in the restaurant I met people in the entertainment business that I started partying with and I was very talented in music, playing 5 instruments and I could sing also. Not to mention that I was a very handsome guy.

Everyone that I knew always told me that I should be a star or that I would be a big star one day. Besides managing the restaurant I would also sell marijuana to all of the other business people, entertainers and athletes that I knew.

The same people that bought marijuana off of me was some of the same stars and business people who later in my life bought cocaine from me, but I'll tell you about that in another chapter of this book.

I had put away quite a bit of money, so when I gave the restaurant back to my father, I took off to LA California in search of fame and fortune. I had quite a few phone numbers of major celebrities so I figured I would be set once I got there, and I was still a very young man.

I also had several big music producers phone numbers, and I called them to tell them that I was on my way to LA. So I left for California but when I got there no one answered their phones. I couldn't get in touch with anybody that had told me to contact them if I ever came to LA.

I got myself a studio apartment in Englewood and went to the University of LA to see about going to college there.

While I was walking to the admissions office I met actress Pearl Bailey, who was going to the University.

She was an older woman but she was attracted to me right away and came onto me. We had a conversation and she took me for a ride around town showing me the sights and then back to my studio apartment. I knew she wanted to come into my place but I didn't invite her in. I just got out of the car and got her phone number from her, I never called her back though.

The next day I awakened and went to go to breakfast at a restaurant but when I got outside the car was stolen. It was a rental car so I figured that I could get another car easily. I called the police and the rental car place but they wouldn't give me another rental car.

Four hours had passed before I found out that they weren't going to give me another rental car and I still hadn't ate breakfast yet. I started walking down the street and it seemed such a far walk in the muggy filthy air of LA.

I stopped at a bus stop and there was a trunk (huge suit case), sitting there. I sat on the trunk while waiting for the bus, and I had this airy feeling of death all around me. The bus came and I took the bus to the down town area to a restaurant to get something to eat.

The restaurant had televisions in it, and the news station was on. The news reporter and police was at the bus stop where I was waiting for the bus and where I was sitting on the trunk. They had opened the trunk up and two dead bodies was chopped up inside of the trunk.

That freaked me out and made me sick to my stomach. I sat down at a table and sitting next to me was Roger and Re-

Run of a popular TV sitcom "What's Happening". They spoke to me and I started telling them of the trunk that I was sitting on that had just appeared on the news.

They invited me to a party that evening in which I went to and had a great time. I met a couple of young ladies there that asked me if I wanted to ride to Las Vegas with them for the weekend, so I went to my studio apartment and packed up my clothes and went with them.

They were super freaks and I had sex with both of them at the same time. It was my first experience like that, and we had sex every day and night the whole time that we were there together. I knew how to hold myself back from cumming, and would go like the energizer bunny. I just kept going and going and going (sex, sex, sex)!

I also gambled at the casinos and made quite a bit of money so when the girls wanted to leave to go back to LA I decided that I would stay in Las Vegas. That trunk ordeal in LA was still freaking me out so I got a studio apartment there in Las Vegas and started gambling every day and night.

One night I was at the crap table rolling the dice, and I was on a roll. I had about $2000.00 in chips and everyone at my table was making money, screaming with excitement. Just as I was getting ready to cash in my chips, Dean Martin and his crew came over to the crap table and told the dealer to give me his roll of the dice.

He even put up the money for me to play. I got on another roll and made another couple of thousand dollars. Dean Martin must have made a couple of hundred thousand dollars off of my roll because he had four stacks of $1000.00 chips filled.

When I finally crapped out, he came over to me to shake my hand and said "The boy's good" gave me one of his $1000.00 chips and he walked away. I forgot what I had come to California for and started chasing women.

I was going to night clubs and chasing different women every other day. I was still very young at 18 years of age and was living it up. I partied so much that I ran out of money and decided to get on the bus and go back to Boston.

I went and stayed with my older sister and her husband and that's when I started going to the gym training to be a professional prize fighter. I soon got tired of partying again and got serious about boxing because I was good at it. I won the New England Welter Weight Championship.

I then joined the United States All Star Boxing team and became a stand in for the 1980 Olympic team. I was very good and I loved boxing, and I trained hard and was fast. I was so fast that I could turn the lights off and jump into the bed before the lights went out.

No one could get to my face because I was so fast and I would protect it. I trained extremely hard on my mind, body and spirit and I won every fight that I had. In 1980 we went to Bosalonia to fight in the Olympics and they boycotted the USA.

Marvin Frazer was a part of the boxing team and he was my friend. We found out that we weren't going to get to fight so we ran off with some German girls to party and have sex. For security reasons they rushed the whole boxing team back to the United States and the plane crashed and killed the whole team.

I missed the plane because I broke training and ran off with some girls. I talk about how oral sex can kill you (a spiritual death) in my book "The Last Chapter" but this time sex saved my life. When I got back home to Boston, I got the royal treatment like I was a hero or celebrity.

I got to do a best buy department store commercial in which I was boxing with a man dressed up in a price tag suit and he knocked me out in the commercial and says "you can't beat these prices". I did a Pizza Hut, Popeye's Chicken, and the Joshlin Family Diabetes commercial. I also did countless of magazine and catalog modeling and as an extra in a few movies.

Willie J

Model, Actor, Performer

REF: Willie Wiggins JR
196 Exchange St.
Millis, MA 02054
1-508-376-8919

CHAPTER 3

Drug Dealing Pimp

Now my sister had a boy friend who was a drug king pin in Boston Massachusetts, and he would pay me $100.00 to $200.00 a day just to ride around with him and be seen with him. I watched and learned how he put cut on his drugs to double his money and then package it up to sell it.

I even made some deliveries some times. He had a twelve man crew who thought that I was his general or right hand man. Well he got shot and killed and I took over his drug business and was making $2000.00 to $5000.00 a day selling drugs.

I was still a Local celebrity so I knew other local stars and when ever entertainers or professional athletes wanted cocaine or marijuana, I was the man that they called. I'm not going to expose their names but I sold drugs to Boston Celtics basket ball players, two Red Sox base ball players, two news anchor men, three talk show host, Countless of performers and entertainers which included singers, musicians, and actors.

I sold drugs to a group of professional Doctors, Lawyers, and Police men and had the commissioner of Boston Massachusetts on my payroll at one time.I would drive to New York and Florida to get Kilos of drugs and bring them back in 3 different cars. It was always an adventure and I got better and better at that job.

I had a crew of 21 men and 12 women and we worked it like a machine. Just like you see in the movies, that shit is true. Life became one big party for me and then came CRACK!! I can remember riding in the car in New York City with two of my men that worked for me, and one of my connections in New York.

He pulled a valve of crack out of his pocket and asked me if I knew what it was. I said no and he explained to me that it was called free base (crack). Cooked up cocaine that people was smoking in pipes.

I said how the hell can you cook cocaine because I knew that it would melt and vaporize in the heat. That's when he took me to his garage and I watched them cook up the cocaine and bring it to a hard rock form known as crack.

They told me how it was going to revolutionize the drug business and bring it to a new level. I went back to Boston and cooked up some of this cocaine into rock form and put it into valves, and sold little pieces of it for $10.00 and $20.00.

It's amazing because when I got back to Boston and told people about it, they had already heard about free basing and wanted to try it. I was the only one around in the South End of Boston who had this free base rock, at least that's what I thought.

I found out that my brother had taken over one of my father's restaurants, and met this girl and started free basing months before I brought crack back from New York. He was getting high so much that it had such a devastating effect on him. He sold all the equipment in the restaurant one day so that he could get more drugs, and neglected the restaurant so much that the restaurant went out of business.

My mother called me and told me what he had did and that he was smoking crack with his new girlfriend. I got some of my crew together and found out where my brother was staying at in the South End with that girl that turned him out to free basing. I went to get him in hopes that I could help to save him but he was too far gone into it.

He wouldn't open the door when I got there, and then the next day he stole my father's car and went to Atlanta City. He eventually came back with a bag full of money, and he paid my father off.

I became so large in the drug game that police told me that the FBI and the ATF was watching me and had me in their system as OC (organized crime). But I was paying the police off and every time they tried to make a move on me I was one step ahead of them.

All the other drug dealers in Massachusetts were coming from different parts of Boston to buy their drugs from me not to mention once again the elite clients of Doctors, Lawyers, Police, Entertainers, and Athletes that were my clients.

I had women of all walks of life wanting me and I took full advantage of it. I had a woman who was an attorney fall in love with me, a radio DJ of a popular radio station (W.I.L.D), a television talk show host of the show (Say Brother), a popular singer who had a record released and countless of women who I slept with just to make them fall in love with me, and I had my way with them.

They would buy me fancy clothes and jewelry. I had them under my power. I soon even met some call girls, strippers and prostitutes that wanted me to be their Mack, Pimp Daddy!! It seemed that the drugs had a strong hold on the whole city and people of all walks of Life wanted to be involved in it.

I met a call girl (prostitute) named Kim who wanted me to be her pimp. I didn't know anything about pimping but I took her in anyways and brought a couple of books written by pimps. One name Silky and I used his guideline for pimping but it came natural for me as all of my sinful ways were.

Remember Satan had a strong hold on me so he made everything so easy in sin for me. I had a drug empire and was now about to get a lock on pimping women. My first Hoe who was bringing me $700.00 to $1000.00 a night, and all I had to do were to manage her mind and emotions.

I wanted to get more girls because I knew that everyone who stayed in the drug business for long periods of time either went to prison or got killed so pimping was a way out for me. I was also now warring against gangs that had formed and was being challenged by other drug dealers who wanted to take me down.

So because of that I just couldn't give it up so easy. I had a reputation to keep. I increased my crew and I made sure that we all were strapped at all times and traveled in packs so we were untouchable.

No one wanted to mess with us because there were rumors that I had ordered the hit on a couple of enemies but that was far from the truth. I never did order a hit or kill anyone and I thank GOD now for that.

I became extremely good at the pimp game, and I was so popular that every time I went down town Boston to the Combat Zone a Hoe was choosing me. When a prostitute would chose you, that meant that she decided to leave the pimp that she was with and get with you.

She would jump in my car and give me anywhere from $500.00 to $1000.00 and I would take her off of the hoe roe (street), and bring her home to groom her to my rules and regulations as her pimp. Then I would bring her to another state to work because most of the punk pimps that lost their girls to me didn't play by the code of the streets or by the pimp code, and I didn't want to have to kill anyone.

I always made sure that I was on point with keeping the peace by any means, and when I couldn't keep the peace I put fear into the person or persons who came against me. In matters of other drug dealers or pimps, I would always find out where their mother lived and have a note sent to her telling her to warn her son that if he and his crew made a move against me that she would be the first one to be killed.

The note warned them that I had a 24 hour watch on their family. I was a very evil man and I had the money and the power to do it. As a Mack (pimp), I met a few pimps that were cool with me. One of them was Boston Red who became friends with me and he was a real OG.

He helped to school me to be a greater Mack and we traveled back and forth to New York together where I met some of New York City's biggest Macks (Pimps). Red knew the pimp game in and out and taught me a lot about it but he had a serious drug problem so our friend ship was short lived.

I traveled all over the country with my girls working my way up to every state from Boston to California & Las Vegas. My girls would tell me of stories about their tricks (customers), how there was those who would pay them large sums of money to piss, shit, or fart in their face.

42

There were some who wanted their balls squeezed until blood popped out of them, and some who wanted to be beaten or choked or kicked in the ass. They would get paid for this sick shit and then come home and give me the money, I became the Mack daddy of the Macks.

I was a professional gentleman of leisure, a drug dealer, a hustler, and con artist.I became a man that would get to know you and take you for everything you got. I would take road trips frequently because as I told you in chapter two I had gotten my associates degree in accounting and I learned all about how the federal reserve bank operated.

I found loop holes in the system in which is the one thing that I won't reveal what I did in this Book But I will tell you that twice a year I worked the banking system from state to state making $5000.00 in each state.

I was also making what my prostitutes was bringing in, and my drug money which was still pumping strong. I would ride around with thousands of dollars in the trunk of my car in shoe boxes.

One year I took six on my girls on a road trip and got to Texas and was at a restaurant sitting outside under an umbrella table along with two of my girls who had a great night of hoeing.

They brought me in $3500.00 each so I rewarded them with lunch with me at a elegant restaurant. As we were sitting there waiting for our food a limousine pulled up and the window came halfway down and a woman was peeping at me through her sun glasses.

My girls told me to go and see what she wanted so I got up and went over to the limo and spoke in a charming voice to her. I introduced myself to her and gave her my business card with simply stated "Professional Gentleman of Leisure". She asked me what that was and I invited her to come and have lunch with me.

She then handed me a card with her name on it as the CEO of a prominent organization. She told me to call her at 4pm so I did. She asked me to meet her for dinner and I did. I told her that I was a business man who owned escort services and a Total entertainment company and she was impressed and wanted to know more.

At the same time I wanted to know more about her so we went to a nearby bar and had a couple of drinks and she told me all about her. She was 33 years of age and married to a 67 year old entrepreneur who owned hotels in Europe and across seas along with real estate in America and a host of other businesses.

She was a multi millionaire and I knew I had hit the jackpot with her. We checked into a room at the Sheraton Hilton Hotel in room 107 and I made love to her like there was no tomorrow.

She had the most beautiful body that I had ever seen. A perfect ten, and the perfect artist conception of a woman. I made her scream and shout so loud that the security came knocking at our door twice.

We had wild and passionate sex that lasted throughout the night and through the morning. When I got through with her the only words she said to me was "I Love You!" She asked me if she could see me again next weekend and I agreed and this went on for 3 months.

I even told her exactly what it was that I did as a living, and she told me that I didn't have to do that anymore and that she would take care of me. I actually thought about it but she was married and I was a Professional Gentleman of leisure, a Pimp, the Mack daddy of the Mack's.

I used the fact that she was married to get out of committing to her and giving up my business. She started giving me $10,000.00 checks every month. One day I told her that I was going back to Boston and I would see her in three weeks, and she told me that she couldn't wait that long. She told me that she loved me so much, and that she wanted to get rid of her husband so that she could be with me forever.

45

I told her that when she divorced him, and had got her share of the money, then we could be together like that. That's when she said to me, "If I divorce him then I won't get anything".

She said "we have to get rid of him", and I asked her what she meant by that? She stated you know! I said what? She said, we have to kill him and hide the body so no one would ever know.

I looked at her like she was crazy, and said no way baby you are on your own with that. She made reservations right then and there for us to meet in Las Vegas for one week. She handed me a small gift box and left out the door.

I opened the box and it was $10,000.00 cash in it and a diamond ring. Like I said, I had hit the jack pot with bagging her. I left the hotel and went to the motel where my Hoes was staying and paged them to call me.

I wanted to call them in so we could hit the road and drive to Las Vegas. They each came with $2000.00 and jewelry for me. The next morning we were on the road on our way to Vegas with $40,000.00 in cash in two shoe boxes.

I had brand new suits and clothes for both me and my girls, and I also had gold chains, bracelets, rings, and watches. We only stopped to get gas and food until we got to Las Vegas. One and half day later we arrived and checked into two different motels.

Prostitution was legal in Las Vegas and the women was gorgeous that worked the strip. My girl's was the top of the line chicks also. I had one that looked like Marilyn Monroe, name Porsche, one named Mercedes, Passion, Strawberry, Jasmine, Ruby, and Sun Shine.

They looked like they stepped out of a glamour magazine. I had them working the hotel bar circuit and the first night they each brought me $2500.00 or more. The next morning I got up and went outside to the news paper machines and I purchased a USA Today News Paper and a local news paper.

Well Rachale the woman who I met in Texas, and who had asked me to meet her there in Las Vegas was on the front page of the USA Today news paper. She had tried to hire a hit man to kill her husband and he turned out to be a Federal Agent.

I didn't have any contact with her for sure after I saw that, and she was sentenced to 20 years in prison. I decided to stay in Las Vegas though because like I said, prostitution was legal and the money was sweet. My girls were hustlers and trained by the best hustler of all, ME!

They knew how to get that money and was bringing it in plentiful! They knew what I liked and I knew what they liked. I was their pimp mack daddy, and business partner, and they were my HOES!

They liked making money and giving it to me, this was the way of the pimp and prostitute. One day inside of a casino, I was playing the crap table and I was on a long great money making roll of the dice.

Everyone at the table was making money off of me rolling the dice. A short bald headed man with thick glasses was betting $1000.00 dollar chips which reminded me of several years back when the first time that I ever went to Las Vegas and I met Dean Martin at the craps table.

Well this little man was betting heavy and was making money off of me. When I finally crapped out he had made a lot of money off of me rolling the dice. He came up to me when it was over and asked me if I wanted to party with him.

Me being the pimp, hustler, con artist and player that I was, I said yes. We went and had a drink at the bar inside the casino and he asked me if I wanted to get some girls to party with us. I knew what he wanted and I said yes.

He then asked me if I knew where to get them. I didn't tell him that I was a pimp but I said yeah and he got a couple of hotel rooms for him and I to party in. He also wanted some cocaine so I called a couple of my girls who liked to get high on marijuana and cocaine and had them meet us at the hotel.

I told him that it was $2000.00 per girl and he gave me $4000.00 so I could give them. I went into the room that he rented for me with my Hoe and told her to stay there in case he needed me and I left.

He went into his room and he partied all night long. He spent $6000.00 that first night with my girls, the hotel room, food, drinks and cocaine. The next day he took us to breakfast and told me to meet him back that evening at the same casino so I did.

We gambled and made out pretty good again, making a few thousand of dollars at the crap table. He then wanted to party again but he wanted two girls for himself he said. I got him two of my other girls and some more drugs and served him all night long.

This went on for 8 days until one day I met him at the casino and we gambled and lost. We left out of the casino and he said that he was leaving town. We walked to the parking lot outside and the police and Feds surrounded us.

There was a helicopter flying over us and they ordered us to put our hands on our heads and kneel to the ground. I asked them what was I being arrested for and they told me to shut up so I did.

When we got to the police station they didn't book me but brought me into a room to question me. They asked me how long I known the man that I was with named Herman. They told me that he was wanted for robbing 18 banks all over the country.

They also wanted to know where all the money was at. I didn't know anything about all of that and I told them that, but they ask me to take a lie detector test so I did, and I passed it so they let me go. The next day he was in all of the news papers.

I remember riding up to the east side of Las Vegas and pulling up into a mini plaza of stores. There were guys walking around with guns out in the open and they were all wearing red shirts and red bandanas.

They were all part of the Bloods, a notorious gang. A couple of guys came up to my car as I was getting out of the car and stood in front of me just staring at me. I said "what's up man" and one of them asked me if I was a cop? I said no I'm a pimp and I need some cocaine for my Hoes.

They looked in my car still holding the guns in their hands and asked me what I wanted. They told me that if I was a cop then they would put one in my head (shoot me). They then told me to follow them, so I got in my car and followed them.

I always kept my gun in my car so I took it from under the seat and put it on my lap. One of them was following behind me and one of them was in front of me and they brought me to the housing projects .

I was cool with it because I had family and friends in both the Orchard Park housing projects, Academy Homes, and the Jamaica Plain Housing projects in Boston Massachusetts. I knew their mentality and how to fit in with them.

One of them came over to my car and told me to wait there so I got out of the car and asked him where was the spots to go clubbing at. I already had knew of a couple of upscale night clubs but I knew that if I was going to be in Vegas and get some respect in the streets then I would have to make myself known among the thugs.

Three bloods came from around the corner of a building and approached me and asked me to show them the money for what I wanted, then one of them told the other one to search me. I had stuck my gun inside my pants under my shirt and he felt it and said a number and they all drew their guns on me and asked me who I was again.

They took my gun and I told them again that I was from Boston and that I was a Pimp and a drug dealer myself. Just then a woman came from around the corner that I had seen on the strip (Las Vegas Blvd). She saw me with my girls and she remembered me pimping at her. (trying to get her for my hoe).

She talked to me that night and told me that she was pimping hoe's and asked me where I was From. We hung out for a couple of hours at a club before going back to check our traps. She was a madam and had six hoe's of her own, and she liked me so she spoke up and told the bloods to chill out and put their guns down.

It turned out that her brother was the leader of the bloods and she told me to come with her. They all followed and she brought me to her brother to introduce me, and get the drugs from him personally.

Her name was Jewel and she was FINE! She told her brother that I was a Mack (pimp) and that she knew me. She told him to hook me up with what I wanted and he did. After I got the drugs we had 15 minute conversation and he invited me to a private party at his house that evening.

I asked Jewel if she was going to be there and she said yes and asked me if I wanted her to pick me up and I said yes. I

I knew that there was going to be trouble, and I had to get out of the area that I lived in, so I started looking for a new house in Henderson Nevada. Jewel wasn't haven't it, she called me and told me that if she couldn't have me then no one else would have me, and told me to buckle up!

A week later I was packing my belongings in boxes with four of my Hoes and two car loads of the Bloods gang pulled up and started shooting up my house. It was just like something out of a movie.

We got down on the floor and I grabbed my gun and put my back against the wall. I waited for them to come in but they never did. I escaped death once again in my life and I left that evening with just a suitcase full of clothes my money and jewelry.

I paid a couple of guys to go to my house and pick up the rest of my stuff and move it to a storage house. Now Denise didn't like the fact that I denied being the father or her unborn child either but she didn't want any harm to come upon me.

She heard about the Bloods shooting up my house and she called me and said that she was on her way over to my house to pick me up. The police showed up first and I told them that I didn't know who shot up my house.

Denise showed up as I was leaving that house that evening with three car loads of Crip members. All of them had guns and cocktail bombs. They told me to get into their car but I refused and they left without me to go into the bloods territory. The police came back to my house just as they pulled off and asked me what was going on and I told them that it was going to be a war.

They told me that they didn't get between the gangs when they were warring and would do a body count when it was over. That was the last time that I ever saw Jewel and Denise because I didn't waste any time getting the hell out of there.

I went to Henderson Nevada and set up shop there. My girls had the names and numbers of their tricks so they did business right out of my home. I still had to watch my back but it was cool there for a while.

It was Christmas time and I gave my girls the weekend off for the first time ever. We sat in front of the fire place talking about our future plans of how we were going to open legitimate businesses, and then the girls started telling me about the John's that they had, and what they were doing to get the money that they were giving to me.

The pimp game was a hell of a hustle and I had to be a tough, slick, cunning, wicked, evil, minded man to do it. A few weeks had passed and it was December 31st, New Years Eve! I got a call from some Real life mafia gangsters that heard that I was doing business in Las Vegas and they told me that they wanted to meet with me.

I ask them why and they told me to just be there at their office. They said that if I didn't meet with them at 12:00 noon then they would see me on their terms. Now I had heard that if you did business in Las Vegas that interfered with the mafia's business, then you had to pay them to do business there.

I ignored them and didn't meet them there and two days later I awakened to four men inside my home standing over me with shot guns pointed at me. I was lying in the bed butt naked with two new girls that I had bumped off of another pimp and the mafia men that was standing over me snatched the covers off of us and told us to get up and get dressed.

Just as I put my pants on, one of them hit me in the face with the butt of his shot gun. I hit and floor and they started kicking me and stomping me. When they were through, they told me to be at their bosses office at 12:00 noon time that next day or they would be back.

I wasn't about to pay them so that next day I packed up and got the hell out of Las Vegas. I didn't stop until I got to Washington DC where we checked into a hotel, and we stayed there for one week.

While in Washington DC one of my girls ended up missing and was found dead two days later in an alley with her throat slashed. I was interrogated by the police along with my other girls and were cleared.

We then we left and went up to New York where I already had some other girls working there. They would send my money to me in Las Vegas faithfully every day by Western Union when I was there.

I would always keep my four best girls there in Vegas and then rotate the other girls back and forth from New York to Las Vegas on a weekly basis. This way they were all satisfied with being a part of the business.

Things started getting crazy because crack had exploded on the scene heavier than ever and my girls started secretly free basing. It was hurting my business both in the drug business and in the pimp game. My Hoes would go to my drug spots and get drugs for free and then run off and get high at the times when they should have been working a John.

Another one of my girls was found dead in New York and my girls now wanted more protection. I hired a couple of more guys that were bouncers in a club to go with my girls on all of their dates and I stopped them from working the bars.

I took each and every one of them off the streets and put them in the escort service business and gave them a body

57

guard for every date. Some of my girls were real classy call girls and some of them were just street hustling Hoes.

Some of them liked to work the bars because they were strippers and knew how to work the bars. So by putting them all together in the escort service business was a big mistake, it took away their hustle.

So now I had to deal with their drug addictions, lack of motivation, and the police coming down on us pimps, and hoe's. I had to worry about the stick up boys, and the fact that some of them ran off and became renegades.

A renegade was a Hoe without a pimp. Because of the fact that I started making more money selling drugs then I was with my Hoe's at that Point, I didn't care anymore about pimping.

It became more of a hazard and liability then of a profitable business. The police moved in on my escort services and arrested me because they said that I was forcing girls to sell their body's which was far from the truth.

I never made any Hoe do anything that she didn't want to do. In fact I never even turned a girl out. They were all prostitutes when I met them and each one of them left their pimp to be with me.

I took great care of them and made sure that they had everything that they needed. But one of my girl's clients was a police detective and he fell in love with her, and wanted her to leave me to marry him.

She didn't want to do that so he formed a unit to take me down. One thing that I was good at, and that was secretly recording conversations with almost everyone I came in contact with for business purposes, and this included the police.

I had that detective telling me that he wanted to have his pick of what girl he wanted when he wanted her in exchange for letting us work his territory. He knew that I paid the police commissioner for that privilege but he didn't care and said that he would bring the commissioner down if he had too.

I had the police commissioner of Boston on tape telling me how much money it was going to take to keep his police off of me, my girls and my crack houses. I had him on tape taking the money.

So when they finally came down on me, and closed my escort services down, they arrested me on white slavery, pimping and pandering, and forced solicitation of prostitution. My escort service was set up legally and I had licenses and documentation to clear me of most of those charges.

I also gave my attorney copies of the tapes, and he went to the district attorney and they dropped the charges off of me in exchange for the original tapes. Now of course I'm not that stupid as to give them the only copies of those tapes, and their not that stupid to think that I would.

Never the less, they dropped all charges off of me, but they cracked down on prostitution and the girls that I had were getting arrested almost on a daily basis. My girls were now full blown drug addicts with the exception of a few but they were too much of a problem for me to continue dealing with them so I gave up the pimp game.

CHAPTER 4

The Fall & Rise of Willie J

Now during the time that I was arrested for white slavery, pimping and pandering, and forced solicitation of prostitution, my attorney gave my case to a female attorney in his law firm named Pam.

She had asked me to meet with her at 11am one morning and I asked her if I could meet her for lunch instead. She accepted the invitation to meet me for lunch and discuss my case, but I didn't give her a chance to discuss anything about the case.

I used my charm and swagger to melt her down like butter and got her to tell me about her personal life. She was single and told me that she didn't have time for socializing because of her work load.

But because it was business she would meet with me that evening. We met at a jazz dinner club called Bob The Chef's restaurant, in the South End of Boston and once again we didn't get to talk much about my case.

I wined and dined her and found out that she hadn't had sex in over a year and that was all I needed to hear from her. We left there and went to her house and she asked me for some blow (cocaine).

Then she broke out with some expensive wine and we sniffed cocaine, drink some wine and had wild and passionate sex all night long. I knew that she hadn't had sex for a year because she was so tight that it felt like a virgin pussy. But I hit it so hard and good that she fell in love with me.

She worked for the law office that I hire and was the one who had received those tapes of the detective and police commissioner taking money from me. I never even had to go back to court, and my charges was dropped that following weekend.

I continued to see her and took her for everything that she had. She had the same name as one of my sisters so I took her credit card and me and my sister went and rented two Thunder Bird automobiles, one for my sister and one for me.

She knew what I was all about so she wanted to keep me happy and provided me with anything that I wanted from her. I continued to sell drugs and every now and then a Hoe would come along and chose me as her pimp and give me her money.

I didn't work her like a pimp though because I was no longer interested in pimping, so they would always leave and get with a pimp that was serious about pimping. My money was in the drug and paper game.

I was pushing paper, checks and credit cards. Now this is something that I won't talk about though. Now my younger brother was a full blown free baser and I would sometimes go over to his house and have him cook up some cocaine for me and he would test it by smoking it.

His girlfriend had two sisters Sherry, and Cherry and they would always come down stairs and flirt with me. I would hit them off with some coke and they would go back up stairs.

61

I would always ask my brother what it was like to free base and he would always tell me that I didn't want to try it because I would get hooked on it. I didn't listen and one day I tried it but it didn't seem like anything special so I tried it again.

The next thing I knew I was going by his house more frequently trying this free base high, and just hanging around for a couple of hours getting high but that was a big mistake. The first law of a drug dealer is to never get high on your own supply.

I became friends with my brothers girl friend and started getting high with her and her sister. I was still hustling and selling drugs on a large scale but I was getting sloppy, careless and not managing my business properly.

Most of my crew members were already addicted to one type of drug or another so my whole operation started falling apart. I didn't care though, I was too busy having fun going to clubs, getting high and having sex with square women.

But I would go over to Sherry's house two to three days out of the week after my main hustling hours which was usually until eleven pm or twelve am. Then I would start free basing cocaine with Sherry, Cherry, my brother, and his girlfriend.

I still had my lawyer girl friend Pam, so I would go there and chill out from getting high for a couple of days and just sell drugs and go back to her house until the weekend. But like I said I was slipping and one day I was at Sherry house bagging up some cocaine and I left a few ounces on the table while I went outside to talk to one of my crew members, and someone stole one of the ounces.

I was partying too much and giving so much money away to friends and family that my stash that I had left upstairs in

Sherry's house was all I had left. So it was a setback for me. I asked my lawyer girl

Pam to give me $2000.00 and she did. She later gave me her bank card and I went and maximized her accounts until I had enough money to get a couple of blocks of cocaine. I then went and stashed the cocaine and brought some of it to Sherry's house and bagged it up.

I cooked half of it up into rock, and half of it I bagged into powder form. I still had customers who liked both and I always treated my customers as human beings and not as crack heads or drug addicts.

They were my life line at this point because I had fell deeper and deeper into the addition myself. I always kept myself up though so that most people that didn't know me would know that I was using drugs. I always wore nice clothes, and kept my personal hygiene up as I continued to out sell all the other dealers in the South End.

CHAPTER 5

224 North Hampton St

It was at 224 North Hampton St in the South End where my biggest troubles and hell started. That was where my younger brother, his girl friend, and her two sisters Sherry and Cherry lived.

That is where I started to free base cocaine at, and where I was selling my drugs at the most. I started getting so high that I neglected everyone and everything thing else in my life.

My lawyer girl friend Pam, had found out that I took her credit cards and almost exhausted her bank account and because I resisted her phone call and was no longer coming around she dumped me, but she didn't press charges against me.

Now all I wanted to do was to sell drugs, get high and have sex with any women that I could freak with. I would stay up for three to four days a week getting high and selling drugs for 24 hours a day.

I was reduced to selling $20.00 and $50.00 rocks of cooked cocaine (free base) which was pure and unlike the man made crack being sold on the streets today. This free base high had changed the game in hustling and most of the pimps, prostitutes, and even drug dealers fell victim to free basing and it destroyed their hustle and lives.

It wasn't long before I was a full blown drug addict. I had to have it every day and all day as long as I was awake. The drug dealers that were small time dealers in the South End knew that I was getting high and didn't like me because their customers were walking past them to come to my spot at 224 North Hampton Street.

This was because I was still a great business man. I would still give the most and the best product for their money. I was selling $40.00 rocks for $20.00 and 16th for $50.00. I sold eight balls for $125.00 when everyone else was selling them for $200.00 or $150.00

I eventually moved into 224 North Hampton Street with Sherry and Cherry and was laying the pipe to Sherry. She fell madly in love with me and got pregnant by me in which she gave birth to me my first son Willie Jamal Wiggins.

The last thing that Sherry and I needed was a child. We were hooked on free basing cocaine, having sex, and making money, and that is all that we wanted to do. Never the less I was a proud papa when Willie Jamal Wiggins was born.

Getting high on free base was the ultimate upper rush and we would get so high that we would need another drug to come down on. So we would take Zanax, Percicets, or any other downer that we could get.

Then we would smoke some weed and have a drink of liquor. We did this 24 hours a day and seven days a week. We were always in an altered state of mind and our lives were based around drugs and getting high.

I still had a hell of a cliental and was now only selling one to two ounces of cocaine a day but the money was still good. I still had jewelry, fine clothes and a car but even that didn't last too long, because I also still had an entourage of family and friends who's drug habits I was supporting.

I would have them wash my clothes, clean the house, run errands for me and whatever else I wanted them to do, they would do it. I was also always getting into fights because other dealers or addicts were always trying me.

They figured because I was getting high that I was weak. But I knew how to fight and I still would always work out so I could be in half way decent shape if I had to fight. I built up my reputation by kicking ass in that neighborhood. My brother was always getting into trouble and then bringing it to me.

He would sell someone some fake rocks or steal a stash from another dealer and then I would have to save his ass, and sometimes I had to save my own ass too. One day some guys came running up to my crib yelling your brother is about to get killed.

I went outside to the back of my building and another drug dealer named Rick and his cousin Carlos had my brother by the shirt dragging him into the alley with guns to his head. The word was that he was a snitch and tried to set them up.

I know the code of the street for snitches and I knew he had some involvement with being an informant but I thought that he had stopped that shit. I did convince Rick and Carlos to let him go though.

Another time I was walking with my brother on our way to get some more drugs and three car loads of Puerto Rican's pulled up on us and my brother ran. I didn't know what was going on but they attacked me with bats and sticks.

I was fighting back but I got hit in the face with a base ball bat. I fell to the ground and they took off in their cars.

66

I got up and started walking back to the house and I got so dizzy that I sat down on some stairs at an apartment building. I was about to pass out when my brother and his friend showed up. They picked me up and brought me to the hospital where I found out that I was stabbed in the back and was bleeding internally.

I remember the doctor pressing down on my back and the blood shooting out like a water fountain. The Dr said that if I didn't get there when I did that I would have died. I found out later that the attack was a result of my brother beating some Panamanians out of their drug stash.

My business was still pumping but the house was getting hot. Undercover cops would sometimes come up to the door to buy some drugs but I would never serve them. I wouldn't serve anyone that I didn't know, so most of the time they would go outside and buy the drugs from one of my crew members or from my brother who would hang outside and sell the drugs that I gave them to sell.

But my brother and most of my crew would always turn in short money to me but I kept on supplying them with drugs and at the same time helping them to pay their rent. The more they turned in short money, the harder I had to hustle and it took more money from my pocket.

It got to the point where sometimes I would get so high and party so much with family and friends that I would end up short for my re-up money and then have to go back to my other hustles to get my re-up money.

When I would run out of drugs the other dealers on the block started standing in front of our place trying to stop my customers from coming up to my spot. They would check to see if we had anything anyways because I was never out of cocaine for more than two days.

I would always tell the other dealers that they couldn't stand in front of my house but when I wasn't there they would go out there anyways. This created a problem because it made my spot hotter than it already was.

I also got into fights with the Lenox Street boys and other gangs in that area that infringed on my territory. Even though I was getting high I still wasn't a punk, I stood my ground.

One day my brother sold drugs to an undercover police officer and got arrested. In order to keep himself out of jail he told the undercover agent that if he let him go then he would tell him who he was selling drugs for and give me up. What he didn't tell the police was that I was his brother. So that evening I was at 224 North Hampton Street, cooking up some cocaine, getting high, and then I heard Sherry yell their coming.

I had taking some percicets, had a couple of drinks and was free basing, so I was so high that I didn't even know what she was talking about. She ran over to the table and grabbed my plate containing an ounce of cocaine and threw it in the sink and tried to turn the water on but the police had shut it off.

She then threw it behind the stove. At that time I heard a big bang at the door and it was the drug unit smashing the door in. I had forgot that I had a eight ball in my pocket that I was on my way to deliver to a customer.

They came in and searched everyone in the house and found the eight ball on me. They then tore up all of the furniture, televisions and VCR's. Right as they was getting ready to take me down stairs to put me in the police wagon, the head of the drug unit Fred Dyer came in.

He was a guy that I used to play basket ball with and had went to school with. He looked at me and said "Willie your brother is a weasel, he snitched you out. He brought me into the bedroom and told me that my brother had sold to an undercover police officer and then snitched me out in order to go free.

Officer Fred then told me that if he knew it was me that they was coming to get then he never would have came up there. He then told me that he would help me and he did. I ended up going to a drug rehab for 30 days and came out a new man, (At least for a while).

I moved in with my sister Lydia when I got out and I called on one of my ex hoes to help me to come up with $5000.00 so that I could get back on with drugs. She got in touch with another one of my ex hoes and I brought them to the Combat Zone, down town Boston and they went right to work for me.

I could always call on them as they never really left me but I left them, but they still loved me though. They stayed renegades working for their selves unless I called on them because they were hooked on drugs also, but I knew how to manage them.

I was a drug dealing pimp so I could give them what they needed to keep them out there working. Now I was clean and sober again and I could think and run my business like I was known for.

I got things popping again and upgraded my customers to a more elite Cliental again. I started going to the night clubs again and met a young lady named Jeanie. She was a doll, very beautiful and I started laying the pipe to her.

She got pregnant and gave me my second son who she also named Willie Wiggins III. I called them Willie #1 and Willie #2 so we would know which Willie we was talking about when we mentioned them.

I stopped having sex with Sherry for about 6 months and would go by just to see my first born son Willie #1 and give her money for whatever he needed. Jeanie was a square girl who held a good job and was very naive to the street life.

She never knew that I was a drug dealer or a pimp or that I was a hustler of any sort. She thought that I was an entertainer and performer and that I was going on the road performing when I wasn't at home.

She was a good woman though and had money in the bank and I was striving to stay clean and sober even though I was still selling drugs. I felt that by being with her I would be able to stay clean and sober so I married her.

Sherry was always a good lay so I would have sex with her from time to time and she ended up pregnant again with my third child Tanika Wiggins. She was a beautiful baby with hazel eyes and such a glow on her face. I was very protective of my children and I would give my life for them even to this day.

I wanted my children around me all the time, Tony, Willie #1, Willie #2 and Tanika, so whenever I was at home with Jeanie I would take Willie #2 out with me in the morning and go down to 224 North Hamton St and spend time with the children.

The problem with that is that Sherry, Cherry, and my old crew and associates was still in the mix of getting high and partying so It wasn't long before I started getting high again, free basing cocaine and selling it from that spot again.

Now I was married to Jeanie but I would stay away from home for three to four days out of the week while selling drugs and getting high with Sherry and my crew. My wife Jeanie soon found out that I was selling drugs, hustling, and getting high.

She reached out to me and tried to get me to get myself together and clean up my act, but I was so caught up into that hustling life style that I wasn't ready to let it go. I ended up leaving Jeanie and she tried so hard to get me to come back to her but I wouldn't.

She finally gave up and it wasn't long before she filed for a divorce. I didn't contest the divorce and agreed to all terms of the divorce in which I'm still paying for to this day. Jeanie stilled loved me though and she stilled tried to get me to sleep with her whenever I came by to see my son.

She still wanted to be with me but I always had a concern for my other children that I had with Sherry. I knew that she was using drugs and I felt that she couldn't take care of my children properly and I was right.

That's why I moved in with her and my children and provided and protected them. There is a saying that "There's no hell like a woman's scorn" and I agree with that!

I was granted custody of my son Willie #2 on the weekends but one day I went by my ex-wife's home (Jeanie) to get my son Willie #2 and she wouldn't let me take him for the weekend as I have been doing for the past few months.

She wouldn't even let me in her house, and she told me that I would never see my son again. I left and went home and when I got home I got a call from a police detective who was in the army with my father and was good friends with him.

He told me that he got call at the police station from my ex-wife Jeanie, and that she told him that I hit her in the head with a hammer and threatened to kill my son, and that I had drugs and guns in my car. She also told him that she wanted to filed a restraining order against me.

The detective told her to come into the police station and file a report and when she did he questioned her about where I suppose to have hit her in the head with a hammer at because she had no marks on her and she had not gone to the hospital.

He told me that he knew that she was lying but that there was nothing that he could do about it. He could not stop her from filing a restraining order against me so she did. He told me to show up at the court the next morning to fight the charges against me and I did, but the judge didn't let me say one word to him.

He let Jeanie speak, and he told me to sit down and shut up. He then granted her a one year restraining order against me to see my son. When that year was up Jeanie went to the court and asked them to extend the restraining order for another year and they did. She continued to do this for five years and I wasn't able to see my son Willie #2 for five years; all because of a false restraining order against me.

I would never hurt a child, never mind my own! As time went on I started getting high again and it got worst and worst because I really didn't care much about my life. I awakened to get high and went to bed getting high. The only decent thing about me was my children. Soon of a later Sherry's apartment was raided by the police, and we was evicted from 224 North Hampton Street and I hit rock bottom as I lost everything that I had.

CHAPTER 6

Street Life, Tragedy, Entertainer

Sherry and I moved into the housing projects and I got my act together and stopped getting high again. I went to work for my father at his restaurant "Walaikums" as I cleaned up my act.

Sherry and I and our children was able to upgrade and move into a three family home in Dorchester Mass. But once again it wasn't long before we started getting high again. One day we was getting high all night long, drinking and drugging and all of a sudden I took a hit of the cocaine and felt like I couldn't breathe.

I couldn't get any air in and I couldn't get any air out of my lungs. I grabbed a can of beer that was on the table in my bedroom and drink some of that thinking it would help but all that did was put more toxicity into my blood stream.

All of a sudden I blacked out and fell to the floor. I remember feeling my soul lift up out of my body and looking down at myself laying there on the floor with Sherry kneeling over me crying.

The strange thing about that experience is that my soul lifted up out of my body and I could see myself laying there. Now my soul didn't have any physical eyes to see with or physical ears to hear with because it is out of my body.

But I tell you the truth, I saw myself laying there with Sherry kneeling over me and I heard her saying "Willie please don't die". I felt myself as I drifted into another dimension and saw darkness on one side and sparkles of light on another side.

I felt like I was in another dimension and I was drifting away from being able to see myself laying there. All of a sudden I wasn't able to see myself or Sherry kneeling over me at all because I was dead.

I felt an evil presence and I felt that I was going to an evil place (HELL). All of a sudden I heard the voice of my son Willie #1 who was about six or seven years of age say to Sherry, "Mommy my daddy dead"!

At that point I was caught in between the dimension of Hell and I said in my spirit "GOD PLEASE DON'T LET ME GO, NO NOT LIKE THIS GOD, DON'T LET ME GO LIKE THIS, MY SON NEEDS ME" and at that point my soul came back into my body and I was still grasping for air to breath.

I told myself to relax and breath and the ambulance came and took me to the hospital where I recuperated at. When I came home from the hospital I was very angry with myself and with drug dealers.

I remember walking to the corner store and a small time dealer on the block saying what's up to me and I ran up to him and grabbed him by the throat and said to him "say something else and I'll rip your throat out".

I was just angry because of what I had become and what had happened to me and I wanted to take it out on any drug dealer that I saw. I decided I wanted to change and to do something to help other drug addicts so I went to school for Psychotherapy for addictions counseling at U Mass of Boston.

Going to school wasn't an easy thing to do because I was working at my Fathers restaurant a few nights a week and those were the nights where the next day in the early morning that I had classes at U Mass of Boston.

I use to go to class and struggle to keep my eyes open only to fall asleep in class. The strange thing about that was that when I would awaken, I would know everything that the professor had talked about and I would always get 100% A's on all my test.

I did an internship at the Framingham Detox in Massachusetts and on the third week of my internship, they offered me a full time job as a substance abuse counselor. I moved my family to the Suburbs in Millis Massachusetts because it was close to the detox treatment facility where I started working at.

Sherry got pregnant again and gave birth to Eunice Martha Wiggins, named after Sherry's mother and my mother. I was working at the treatment facility during the day and at my father's restaurant on the weekend nights.

One night I came home from the restaurant at 4am and took a shower and got in bed and started to fall asleep and Sherry awakened with a scream. I jumped up and Sherry was yelling that something was wrong with my baby Eunice.

I looked at her and her eyes was pushed in and she looked like she was dead. I grabbed her and her body was limp like a rag doll. I told Sherry to call the ambulance and I started giving Eunice CPR.

The ambulance came and rushed her to the hospital and I rode in my car behind them. The hospital had to pump Eunice stomach and put tubes through her mouth to her stomach.

It turned out that Sherry had let one of her friends son stay at our house for the weekend and he was a manic depression child who was on medication for his mental illness. He had a pouch with his pills in it and they were coated with a sweet coating for kids. Eunice got a hold of it and ate them like they were candy. That was a very scary time for us as we almost lost our child, but she fully recovered.

Eunice, Willie#1, Tanika and Marissa

During my time working at the detox treatment facility, I counseled judges, lawyers, policeman, professional football players, basketball players, and people of all walks of life. But mostly it was the very same people who I sold drugs to for years that came into the detox treatment facility to get clean and sober.

People would confess their most inner secrets to me and then break down and cry like a baby, (both men and women alike). I was good at counseling too and gained a lot of respect from people all over the state of Massachusetts.

One day the police brought a man into the treatment facility for alcohol and substanceabuse treatment. He was a homeless man living in the streets and was in very bad shape. I use to do group counseling and individual counseling and after five days of that man being there in the detox program he came out of shock and into the group meeting to participate.

He told the group and me that he was once a doctor and owned a large incorporation and that his wife had died in an automobile accident in which he was driving and he walked away from all his riches and family and had been living on the streets for two years.

He told us of all the famous people that he knew and was his friends but no one believe his story and even I found it hard to believe because he was in bad shape, physically, mentally and spiritually.

Five days later we got a call at the detox facility from Senator Ed Kennedy. He stated that the man was a friend of his that grew up with him and his family, and that they had been looking for him for two years.

Later that day Michael Kennedy came to the detox with his entourage to pick him up and they left. Sherry was still my girl and the mother of my children Willie # 1, Tanika and Eunice, and one day I asked her what she wanted from me.

She had always been loyal to me and never bothered me about much of anything that I did, even all that other women that I had. She told me that she wanted to be my wife and I figured that we was living together so getting married wasn't a bad idea so I told her that I would marry her.

I remember sitting at the kitchen table in Millis Massachusetts and talking to GOD about getting the money that I needed for the big wedding that we had planned. I was short on cash about $700.00 and I knew that everyone in my family was broke so I couldn't ask GOD for the money.

Even though I knew nothing of Jesus Christ I asked God for the money that I needed in the name of Jesus Christ. I went to the corner store and brought some lottery scratch off tickets and I lost.

I went back to the store and brought some more tickets and lost more money. Now I was digging a deeper hole for myself. I was now $900.00 short because I had spent $200.00 on scratch tickets trying to win because I had been lucky in the past, winning the money that I always needed.

I continued to buy those scratch tickets that day until I got down to my last $100.00 and I sat there at the kitchen table and I said the words "IN THE NAME OF JESUS CHRIST IF IT IS MEANT FOR ME TO MARRY SHERRY THEN LET ME WIN THE MONEY THAT I NEED TO GET MARRIED GOD".

I pursued to scratch the ticket and I won $20,000.00 instantly. I jumped up and went to the store to ask them were I needed to go to cash it in. I went to the lottery commission and the government took $6,400.00 in taxes off of the top and gave me $13,300.00 which was the amount that I needed so we planned our wedding and got married. I

Took Sherry to the Bahamas for our honey moon and we had a great time. Soon after that another man came into the detox name Big Mike. He didn't seem to have any drug problems and didn't look like it either.

He told me that he had just gotten out of prison, and that as a part of his release he was told that he had to go to a treatment facility to get clean and sober. He said that the reason for this was that he was selling drugs in prison, and got caught with drugs but told them that he developed a drug habit inside the prison in order to keep from doing more time.

His release was due and they sent him there to the detox to complete that program before he could be completely released. One day me and big Mike was talking in a private counseling session and he told me that he was a Rap Hip Hop artist who took the blame for his father and went to prison.

He said that he had written a lot of material and wanted to get it published. I asked him to let me hear some of his material and he started rapping for me. He recited his lyrics with such passion, grace and perfection that I knew he was a natural born star.

I had started writing and working on some hip hop songs myself but I couldn't rap, I could sing and play seven instruments. I told Big Mike that I could use him on my album so when he got out of the program we hooked up and started practicing our music together.

We hit the studio and recorded a three song maxi single titled Positive Example. I had studied and learned all that I could about the music business so I set up my own label and publishing company called Strong Roots Productions.

At that same time my job as a substance abuse counselor at the treatment facility started becoming very stressful. I remember sitting there at my desk listening to clients all day telling me of their problems and I felt like my head was going to explode.

I was absorbing everyone's pain and suffering because I had really cared and had a passion to want to help them. I was sitting there though, saying to myself as I was listening to a client, "please leave, get out of my office, I don't want to hear this no more" It really felt like my head was going to explode. That next day I put in my two week notice in to quit. There is a statistic that says that psychiatrist has the highest rate of suicide than any other profession.

$\mathcal{P}$ ositive $\mathcal{E}$ xample

For Bookings or more information contact: Strong Roots Productions

81

I soon became a member of ASCAP (The American Society Of Authors, Publishers and Composers), and they voted me onto the chairmen of the board. I was asked by ASCAP to come to the first chairman of the board meeting of the year in New York and I did.

I remember seeing a very young and skinny Sean Combs Aka P Diddy. He wasn't known yet and was just starting out in the music business. I believe he was also voted on the chairmen of the board and we spoke briefly, but I didn't stay to find out because I got a emergency call from Big Mike.

He told me that he needed me to come to the hotel right away because the police was there because he didn't have his key to the room and it was in my name. The hotel clerk wouldn't give him a key so he started raging on the clerk and they called the police.

I had to get there to straighten things out so that they wouldn't arrest Big Mike. I never did go back to any of the ASCAP board meetings in which would have created major opportunities for me and my publishing & record company, Strong Roots Productions.

So I blew another chance at great success. I did get distribution for our maxi single in Sam Goody's, Strawberries, and Skippy Whites Record stores. I also got picked up on a show festival tour as the opening act for major stars like The Force MD's, The Fat Boys,, Kurtis Blow, and Grand Master Flash and the furious five.

That tour lasted for six months and then we did the New York and Boston Music festivals in those states, and also a lot of club performances all over the country. After about one year and a half the gigs stopped coming in and Big Mike and I both went back to hustling, selling drugs to keep up our new found life of luxury.

As time went on things were changing dramatically in the drug business. New Jacks were coming up who were gang bangers that wanted to make names for themselves and young people were killing each other every day like they had simply gone out of their minds.

Because of drug related deaths and association with it I lost two sisters, a cousin, my uncle, and two best friends all within less than two years. Most of my crew was either already dead or locked up in prison.

I know now that it was only the mercy and grace of GOD that I escaped jails, institutions or death. One day I was in New York City with Big Mike and we were at a night club where we met three women.

We partied together at the club for a couple of hours and then went back to my place to party some more. One of the women was sitting in my lap at the kitchen table and one was sitting on Big Mikes lap on the couch.

The other woman was standing in the window behind the curtains talking to someone on the cell phone. We were drinking, and smoking weed, and the girls were sniffing cocaine that we gave them.

I had giving them tee shirts to put on, and the two women that were sitting on me and Mikes laps stripped naked and put the tee shirts on. The woman that was in the window didn't put on a tee shirt and all of a sudden the door bell rang.

Mike and I were so indulged with the two women that were sitting on our laps that we didn't pay attention to woman talking on the cell phone at the window and to who was ranging our door bell. So when the door bell ranged the young lady on the cell phone at the window shouted I'll get that and we let her go to the door to answer it.

Came in and had guns drawn on us and told us to "STAND UP AND KEEP YOUR HANDS TO YOUR SIDE! They made the two young ladies lay down on the floor and lined me and Big Mike up side by side, shoulder to shoulder.

They started patting down my pockets and took $750.00 out of my pocket. Then one of them snatched my gold chains off of my neck, ripping my skin. They then told Big Mike to take off his thick gold chain dope rope, and then they went to pat down Mikes pocket and Mike pushed one of the robbers hands away and he shot Mike in the head.

I was standing, shoulder to shoulder with Big Mike and his brains and flesh flew all over my face. Flesh and blood was dripping down my face and the robbers dropped most of the gold jewelry and money as they ran down the stairs.

I started trying to stuff Big Mikes brains back into his head and took my shirt off to use it to try to stop the bleeding but he was already dead. The other two women were yelling and screaming and tried to pick up the telephone to call the police.

I knew that I had drugs and guns in my safe in the bedroom so I told them to put the telephone down so I could get the drugs and guns out of the house. Then I told them to call the police.

Me and the girls were interrogated and the detectives told me that they knew what I was doing and that if I sold any more drugs in the state of New York then I would go to prison for a very long time.

CHAPTER 7

Entertainment, Opportunity, & Failure

After Big Mike got killed and I was cleared with the law, I knew that it was time for me to change. I knew that I couldn't live like that anymore and that I had to make a change in my life.

I had lived a life of crime traveling from state to state pushing paper, and embezzling money from Incorporations that I worked for. I was working bank accounts, credit cards, selling drugs, pimping, setting up robberies, being a gigolo and coning as many people as I could possibly con.

So tired of all of this and wanting a better way of life, I packed up my bags and I moved to Florida. I had associates that I knew in the hustling and thug life that had homes in Florida.

They would come to Florida to get away from their everyday life of the hustle and bustle of the street life. So my first year in Florida I just hung out and thought about everything that I wanted to do with my life.

On the weekends I would go out and party and enjoy the sun shine states beaches, women, and tropical life. I enjoyed working out every day so I kept myself in great shape and I started working hard on my mind, body and spirit.

After about a year I brought my wife Sherry and my children Willie #1, Tanika, Eunice and Marissa to Florida to live with me. I wanted to be a good husband and father to my children now.

I started looking for a job and found a job as a manager of Boston Market restaurant in Florida. We moved into a home in Lauderhill Florida in Broward county and were living a decent life.

Our neighbors were Christian people and would invite us to their church all the time.One day I accepted their invitation and they came over to my home and gave me a bible. I opened up that bible and begin to read it for the first time.

I didn't know anything about Jesus Christ but something about that book made a lot of since to me and caught my attention. I still had a lot of demons in me and one day Sherry wanted to get high again and I gave into her temptation and went and got us some cocaine to cook up and free base.

It was one of the worst things that I could have done in Florida. I had a decent job as the manager of Boston Market restaurant and I was a good manager and I had started getting high again.

I was fighting against it once again, and Satan started having his way with me. I was able to stop for a few weeks at a time but then I would go out with some friends to a club and we would drink and get high.

One day I decided that I was going to take my family to the Golden Heights Baptist Church in Fort Lauderdale and get all of us baptized and we did. I was trying everything that I could to stop getting high but I never went to a drug rehab or detox.

My wife and I stayed clean and sober for a few more weeks after being baptized but then gave into the devils dope. Sherry and I would get high all night long and then we would both go to work high the next day.

The really bad thing about that was that our children suffered the most because we never spent any real quality time with them. As I reminisce and write about it I feel discussed.

One day a friend of my ask me to rent a car for him and he would pay me up front with cash for it. I rented the car for him but I didn't put him down as the driver. I rented it with my credit card and under my driver's license.

Well he took the car and I never heard anything from him again. My credit card kept on paying for it until my card was maxed out and canceled. One night I was on my way to get some drugs and I got pulled over by the police in the drug area of Hollywood Florida.

They ran my license plate and found out that I had a warrant for my arrest for not turning in that automobile that I rented for my friend. Sherry billed me out of jail and I made it to work the next day at Boston Market.

I was also driving a rental car at the time that I was arrested for the rental car that I rented for my so called friend. They took that car when I was arrested and I had no way to get back and forth to work and I had no more money saved up to buy a car.

I needed a car to be a manager of that restaurant because as a manager, you have to make daily bank runs, and go to other restaurants to pick up or drop off inventory. It was also far away from where I lived so I had to do something about this.

So I planned to set up the restaurant to be robbed. I knew everything that I needed to know about doing this so I set it up perfectly with another associate of my.

He was to come into the restaurant 5 minutes prior to us closing wearing a hooded jacket to cover his face and walk straight to the men's rest room. Then he would come out ten minutes later wearing a ski mask after we were closed, and tell everyone to get into the walk in refrigerator.

He would then put the gun on me to make me cover the two video cameras in the store and open the safe to give him the money which was usually around four thousand dollars. Well when the night came for him to come and do the robbery, he never showed up.

I waited until all of the employees were gone and I decided that I would do it myself. I had brought some clothes that I had in the old used rental car that I had, and I changed my clothes into some old dirty pants, a shirt and a hat.

I covered my face with a scarf and then I covered the video cameras and went to the back of the store and took the money out of the safe and put it into my car. I called the police and reported that I had been robbed at the restaurant and they came and took the report.

The next day they asked me to come to the police station to make a full report and give another account of what happened. I did and they asked me to take a lie detector test but I refused.

Boston Market told me that because I refused to take the lie detector test that I was fired. Two days later I got a call from the detectors stating that they need to talk to me but I didn't show up at the police headquarters.

I had another check coming to me from Boston Market and I called them to tell them that I was coming to get my check and they told me to come and get it. When I got there the detectors was in the back of the store waiting on me and arrested me.

I was brought to the police station and booked for robbing the restaurant and filing a false report. I still had the automobile grand theft charge pending against me and I was out on bail for that so my bail was revoked and denied.

I was sent to the Broward County jail in Fort Lauderdale Florida to wait for my court date. I sat there for three months waiting for that court date to come up. Finally I went to court and they gave me two years of probation for what I did.

Sherry and I decided to move to South West Florida where some of our other friends from Boston had moved too so we packed up our belongings and moved to Port Charlotte Florida. I had transferred my probation to there and we moved into a big 4 bedroom house.

Once again, it was my children who suffered the most because when I moved them to Florida things started getting bad for me. I was fine before Sherry came to live with me, and as soon as she came she wanted to get high so we did and that one night was all it took to get me started again. Satan still had a strong hold on me but it was a temporary condition.

We got evicted from the houses that we rented three times and twice from the condo units that we rented. Each time that we got evicted we had to move our children into a different area in Florida.

Three of those times we had to transfer them to different schools. Now this had a psychological effect on them because they moved away from their friends and had to make new friends each time.

When my son and daughter Willie #1 and Tanika was in middle school in Pompano Florida, they were both put into advance special classes for advanced students. My son was actually put into a class with other high school and college students so that when he graduated from high school he would have already had two years of college in.

90

All of this was taken away from them because of Sherry and my drug addiction and the strong hold that Satan had on us still. I still had skills as a hustler and I knew how to market and sell myself very well to any company that I wanted to convince that I was the man for the job.

Well when we moved to Port Charlotte Florida, I got a job as the manager of Eckerd's Pharmacy, a southern Franchise organization. I was working 60 hours a week on a very low salary for the amount of work that I was doing but I was really trying very hard to get my life in order.

I worked there for a year and did a great job. I even stopped getting high for about six months. After one year of being there, Eckerds Pharmacy sold their business to CVS Pharmacy.

After that I went to work as a manager of Wendy's Hamburgers fast food restaurant. I was a good manager and had very good leadership skills. I got promoted very quickly and won awards for having the best customer service at a fast food restaurant in SW Florida.

Wendy's Inc. recognized me as an example of how to provide great customer service to their customers. Then all of the women started coming at me strong that worked there and I started having sex with other managers and employees.

Most of them liked to get high and drink so that led me back into getting high again. I still was able to maintain my status as a good manager but I started selling drugs over the counter and out of the fast food window there.

I gave a job to a guy that was in a work release program from prison and we became good friends. He turned out to be a big drug dealer in SW Florida and had big connections so I was able to get my drugs at the lowest price whenever I wanted too.

Even without any money he would front me. I was making money working there at Wendy's as the manager and as a drug dealer. I had money, women and drugs once again. Sherry still didn't bother me about nothing that I did.

She just enjoyed getting high, driving nice cars and living that crazy lifestyle. While working at Wendy's I hired a young man named Jason who turned out to be a great hip hop rapper with a awesome deliverance and voice.

My son Willie #1 started rapping at a very early age and writing his own lyrics and songs. I connected them together and started grooming them for stardom.

Music has always been a great love of mine and I never put it down even to this day. I got some beats together and we brought some beats off a recording artist named Nate. I worked hard with them for two years diligently, until I felt that they was ready to make a CD in a recording studio, and then I brought them into the studio to record.

We recorded two songs and then Jason aka (Bullet) brought to me another young man named young Jay. He had a unique style that complimented the group so we brought him into our family.

We named the group New Breed and my son Willie called himself Bombz and was the main rapper of the group. We continued to record in the studio until we finished eleven songs and then I started to look for female dancers for the group.

That's when my son's girlfriend Francine Aka Cina was brought into the group and she had friends who could also dance. Everything was fallen into place and for once I really felt that something special going on.

92

I was still hustling on the side just to pay for all the studio time that I was paying for. It cost me $65.00 an hour to record and since I was a determined to do it right, I spent an average of 5 to 8 hours at a time on one song in the studio.

My new found friend Alton got out of the half way house that he was in from prison and we started to hang out on the weekends. He got out of prison and went all out for money, women and drugs.

I call it Satan's big three, (money, women and drugs). It's how Satan gets a strong hold on us and keeps us under his strong hold. I started hanging out so much with Alton and not going home at night.

I was still on probation and every month they would call me into the lab for drug test but I would always stop getting high for four days and then take a drink of detox to clean my system out so I always passed the drug test.

I started missing days at work and the area director started hearing about all the activities that I was involved in at the restaurant and I was warned to get myself together and stop whatever I was doing.

They really liked me there and didn't want to fire me but I continued to get worst and stopped caring about that job so they did fire me one day. Once again by getting high on cocaine, drinking, hustling and chasing women, I neglected my children and my wife and job and all my responsibilities.

I used to come home and my daughters Tanika, Eunice, and my niece who I raised as my daughter Marisa would want to play with me. I would yell at them and send them to their room so I could get high with their mother Sherry.

93

This had such a damaging effect on my daughters that one day I was on the couch trying to recuperate from a night of drinking and drugging and my daughter wanted to talk to me and I yelled at her and sent her to her room. A few minutes later she came out of her room with a look of fear and rage on her face.

It was a look that I would never forget. She grabbed a long kitchen knife and walked by me and went into her bed room. I got up and followed her to her bed room but she had locked her bed room door.

I busted it open and she was in her bathroom with that door locked and I started screaming at her to open that door. She was crying hysterically and I knew that something was seriously wrong.

I busted that door open and my daughter was cutting her wrist. She wouldn't give me the knife and had it on her wrist. I grabbed the knife from her but she kept on saying that when I go to sleep that she was going to kill herself.

I called the hospital to get help and they sent the police. She was only 12 or 13 years of age and they came into my house and grabbed her as if she was a criminal. She was struggling with them and one of the officers threw her down and put his knee on her Head.

That's when I went off and tried to get to him, and two officers grabbed me. They carried my daughter out picking her up by her arms and legs while she was in hand cuffs. She was brought to the hospital where she was heavenly sedated and I went there and cried like a baby seeing my daughter like that.

After a couple of days of observation I was allowed to bring her back home. That was the saddest time of my life and

I vowed to change at that time. I had to change to save my children. Time passed and she made a full recovery.

Sherry worked as a Certified Nurses Aid and was now working long hours. It was hurricane season and the news channels had broadcasted that a hurricane named hurricane Charley was going to hit Tampa.

We lived 1 ½ hour away from Tampa in a town called Port Charlotte. Four hours later the news station broadcasted that the stormed turned and was going to hit Fort Myers which was 30 minutes away from us.

But at the last hour we were told that the hurricane was going to hit Port Charlotte we're we lived. It was a category four hurricane, and we were told to find shelter and get ready for the worst storm to ever hit South West Florida.

We had no idea what was about to happen but I went out and brought cases of water, batteries, flashlights, and food that was already prepared, and a couple of ice coolers with six bags of ice that I put in the freezer.

Sherry was at work and told me that her job offered her double pay to go to the shelter out of town with the nursing home that she worked for so she did. I was home with my children when the storm started approaching slowly.

The winds had picked up and we went to the door and stood outside for a moment. It didn't seem that bad at first but all of a sudden it started raining and the wind picked up another notch.

The rain started coming down heavier but was blowing completely sideward's. I saw a flock of about 50 birds being blown sideward's and then all of a sudden they were taken by the wind straight up in the air and tossed around like paper.

Me and my children was standing outside at the door to our house while this was going on and I yelled at them to get into the house. I tried to close the door but the wind was so strong that I had to use all of my strength to close it.

We went upstairs and were looking out of the windows and the phone ranged. It was Jason (Bullet) on the phone. He lived in the next town up from us in Punta Gorda Florida.

As we was talking he stated that he heard something banging on his roof. All of a sudden he yelled on the phone "Oh shit, the roof just came off". Before he could say anything else the phone went dead and the lights went out.

The electricity was off and the eye of the storm was over us. I gathered my children away from the windows and we huddled in our livings room, and waited for the storm to pass. When it was over with my children and I went outside to look around and it looked like a war zone.

It looked like someone had dropped bombs on us. All of the houses around us were destroyed accept our house, and the trees were gone. Some of the huge trees were pulled up out of the ground and the whole ground came up and you could see down into the earth.

Every light pole and telephone pole was down and there were electrical wires down everywhere. I told my children to come back inside and we went upstairs. I went into my bedroom to use the toilet and when I came back they had left the house.

I got worried and went looking for them but I couldn't find them. Thirty minutes passed and they hadn't come home yet so I was on my way to find the police to help me find them when they came home all covered in mud.

They told me that they had fallen into a ditch filled with mud that was above their heads. From what they told me, it was only by GOD'S grace that my son Willie #1 was able to get out of there and save the rest of them.

The next day we got into my car and we was going to drive to my son's girl friend's house Cina who was also the dancer of the group and then we was going to go to Jason's house to make sure that they were ok.

It was so much destruction that we couldn't get down any street because of the trees and downed light poles and destroyed houses that blocked the roads so we turned back. We went into the house and played games, listened to the radio and ate food.

The next day we went walking and it was so depressing to see so much destruction and people standing around their destroyed homes waiting for help. I heard a broadcast on the news that everyone was to stay in their homes and if you were caught outside after 7pm then you would be arrested.

I had a cell phone but it was dead so I couldn't call anyone yet. Five days later the US Army and FIMA came to bring water and supplies and stop the looter's who was going into what was left of the stores and taken things.

People had signs up that said that you would be shot on sight if caught on their property. Finally we were able to make it up to Jason's house and it was completely destroyed. Jason and his family was no were to be found and It struck me hard because the last thing I heard was him yelling on the phone that the roof came off and then phones went dead.

I inquired about Jason and his family with the state police and they put in for a search for them. One day later Jason and his mother showed up to my house and asked me if he could stay with us for a while because they had lost their home.

I took Jason in and treated him as my own child. This is when my son Willie #2, Jason and myself really bonded and practiced writing our music and music arrangements. We were out of electricity for more than a month and as the days went on we had to stand in longs lines for food and water. Having experienced hurricane Charlie is something that I hope I never have to go through ever again.

CHAPTER 8

Time for Change (New Beginnings)

I was putting together a plan for my group "New Breed" and I had it all planned out from the marketing and promoting to the recording, performing, concerts and show productions to the distribution of the CD'S. But during all this time I was still on probation and it was the first week of the month when I had to go and report to my probation officer.

They never had drug tested me before and I had smoked some weed three weeks prior to going in, and all of a sudden they wanted to drug test me. This caught me off guard and I didn't want to piss but they told me that if I didn't then they would violate me right then and there so I pissed in the cup and came up with a dirty urine.

That violated my probation and I was sent to the Broward County jail for 45 days while waiting for my court date and sentencing. I really wanted to do the right thing in my life, and me and the boys

New Breed worked hard at being prepared for the opportunity for success, and now they had to be put on hold. While I was in jail I was waiting on a settlement from a law suit and one day Sherry came to see me in jail and told me that my lawyer had called me to come in and get my money.

99

I told Sherry that I was going to give her the right to get my money and that I wanted her to give $1,500 to each one of my children and that she could take $2,500.00 for herself, and I told her to bring $1000.00 to the jail, and put it into my commissary account.

Then she was supposed to put the rest of the $5,000 into my bank account but I never heard back from her again. She got the money and then wouldn't accept my collect calls, and took my money and moved to another part of Florida.

I was in jail with no bail and had no way to contact anybody because her phone number was the only phone number that I remembered. Now of all times she decided that she had enough and didn't want anything to do with me anymore.

I didn't care so much about that but I wanted my money! When the time came for me to go to court they offered me a plea bargain but I refused it and so I had to wait in jail for another 45 days before going back to court.

I spent that time reading the Holy Bible, working out, and praying to GOD for mercy and a better way of life. I prayed to GOD that HE would allow me to feel HIM and to let me know that HE was there.

When the time for me to go to court came, I was released on one year of house arrest followed by 2 years of probation. The problem was that I had given my address as the house where Sherry and I lived before she left, and I had no place to go.

My cell phone was dead so I couldn't even get any phone numbers off of it. I knew I had a buddy name Rob who lived in Lauderhill so I knew that if I could make it to his place and he was in town then I would be straight.

CHAPTER 10

13 Months (The Anointing)

When I got to the Sarasota county jail, there were detectors from two other counties waiting to talk to me. They gave me no bail and said that they were looking for me for three years.

They brought me into an interrogation room and showed me pictures of my associates, my brother and my girlfriend. The first two detectives was from Sarasota county and charged me with 4 first degree felonies; insurance fraud for filing for insurance under the drivers license that I took for my brother, filing for a drivers license under a false name, and taking the driver's test under a false name, and then filing for a title under a false license.

The detectors wanted me to turn my brother in for conspiring with me to take his driver test for him but I didn't. I told them that I did it without his knowledge just to keep him from being arrested.

The next two detectors were from Charlotte County and they charged me with 3 counts of credit card fraud, and the other two detectors was from Fort Myer's (Lee County). They charged me with 4 first degree felonies, of trafficking stolen jewelry, pawning stolen jewelry, using a false ID to pawn stolen jewelry, and grand theft of $70,000 worth of jewelry.

They had pictures of associates of mine that were involved in the theft of the stolen jewelry and they showed them to me and wanted me to identify them and snitch them out, but I told them that they had nothing to do with it, and that I did it all myself.

They told me that if I didn't tell them who my associate where and if I take the blame for them that I was going to go away to prison for a very long time, but I refused to snitch on my associates and I yelled at them to get me a Bible.

All I could think about at that time is that I wanted a Bible. I had lived a life of sin and came to Florida to change my life and it was a struggle trying to change but I thought I was doing pretty good compared to how I used to be and the things that I used to do but none the less, I still committed crimes by breaking the law.

The thing about it is that out of all the terrible things that I did in my life, I came to Florida to change my life and got jammed up for trying to help others. Nothing that I did was for the purpose of total selfish gain.

I took the driver's license test to help my brother Marcus and I applied for those credit cards with my own social security number and name but they was manipulated. I assisted in the jewelry theft to get money to help a friend as well as myself.

But none of that compared to any of the crimes that I had committed in the past and never got caught for. Now I was about to pay the price for all that I did in my life and I was afraid. I knew that I was going to go away for a very long time.

The detectors asked me to confess in writing and on tape of the charges that they charged me with so I did. At that point I didn't even care about confessing. I just didn't want anyone else who was involved in everything to get arrested and I just wanted to get it all over with.

After I confessed everything on tape and written confessions, the detectors told me that I was looking at 20 years in prison for all of this. I was brought to a jail pod and just told to find any cell to go into.

I walked up to each jail cell and they all had two or three inmates in them except two of them. I went into one of them and there were commissary items on one of the bunks and a inmate sleeping on the other bed.

I started removing the items off of the bed and the inmate yell "what the fuck was I doing". He told me that if I didn't put his stuff down that he was going to kick my ass.

I yelled back at him and told him to "get up out of bed and move his stuff right now or that I was going to snatch him out of the bed and kick his ass and that was real". He got out of his bed and he smelled like a dead man, I know that smell when I smell it.

He looked at me and the smell on him made me furious. I walked up to him and told him to "get his stuff off of the bed right now or I'm going to beat him like he stole something from me".

He must have felt that I was serious and meant every word that I said because he started taking his stuff off of that bed. Other inmates heard me yell at him and had come out of their cells to see what was going on.

After he took his stuff off of the bed I said to him in a load voice, "now that you took you stuff off of the bed I don't want to stay in here with you. I told him that he smelled like shit and needed to jump in the shower". He stated back to me that he don't take showers and he meant that!

I walked over to the only other cell that had only one guy in it and went in the cell and set myself up. The inmate in that cell was cool. He introduced himself and we had a decent conversation.

He told me of the gang that was in that pod and was basically running it. I wasn't worried about that and it didn't scare me at all. I immediately went to reading my Bible and working out. Breakfast was at 5am so I would get up and 4am and do a one hour work out before breakfast every morning.

Then after breakfast I would take a shower and go and clean my cell. The dining was in our pod and after breakfast it was always a mess. The inmates wouldn't clean it for a couple of days at a time until the guards came in with trustees to clean it and then the inmates would dirty it up right away again. They were like savages in there.

They would sit on the tables to watch TV, and they all smelled and didn't shower daily. Right after breakfast everyone would go back to their cells and go back to sleep. Usually I would go back to my cell and study my

Bible and get my prayer on. One morning I got tired of being in there in all the filth so I asked the guards for some cleaning supplies and I cleaned the whole pod including the showers. Then I took a shower and went to my cell and did my Bible study and prayer.

After lunch time the inmates would trash the place again and then go to their cells and take a nap or just hang out in the trashed dining hall playing cards or plotting on the new weak inmates that came in.

I continued to clean, and they continued to trash the place, right after I would clean every day. One day I spoke up to them and told them to stop trashing the place and that it was our home for now.

Everyone started cussing at me and told me that they didn't tell me to clean up. They just laughed and joked about it and told me to go and fuck myself. I went into my cell and I prayed to GOD to hear my prayer.

I asked GOD to make them stop trashing the place and to make them start helping me to clean. I told GOD that I was tired of cleaning behind those grown men, and that I needed them to start cleaning up behind their selves.

The next morning I got up and did my workout and the leader of the gang, a guy named Charles was in the dining room where I work out at. He came up to me and said that he wanted to work out with me from now on because he wanted to get in good shape.

He knew that he was also going away to prison. So we worked out and then breakfast was served and we ate breakfast. After breakfast, the place was trashed again and I started cleaning up as I always do. All of a sudden I heard Charles telling his crew to get their asses up and come out and help the Rev clean. (that's what they had started calling me "Reverend Og Willie J").

So 8 of them came and cleaned that morning with me. GOD had heard my prayer for help to clean, and sent Charles and his crew to help me. It may not sound like such a big deal but I'm telling you that the last thing on Charles and his crew minds were cleaning, never mind helping me to clean.

Later that day after lunch, everybody in the pod was trashing the place again and had thrown food all over the walls and floor and Charles and his gang made everyone get back in there and clean up.

From that day on, for the rest of the time that I was there it stayed clean. Two weeks later the guard came to me and asked me if I wanted to go to what was called the GOD pod. That was a new part of the jail where professors from different universities, and Pastors of all denominations of different churches came and taught the inmates.

They taught about the Christian way of life, and would study the Bible all day in different classes. I accepted that and was transferred there later that evening.

There is 24 hours in a day and I'm telling you that in all the time that I spent in jail (13 months), I would work out for one hour, eat clean and shower and then I did would study and pray and meditate on GOD until I couldn't keep my eyes open no more.

It must have been the second week in the GOD pod when I was sitting on my bed one day and I was talking to GOD, asking HIM to be with me and to let me feel him. I couldn't feel HIM there and I wanted to know that He was there.

I asked GOD to be with me for the rest of my life and to let me work for HIM for the rest of my life. I said to GOD that "I'm putting in my application for employment to work for you for the rest of my life GOD"I then heard the voice of the lord say to me "LIVE BY MY COMMANDMENTS AND I WILL BLESS YOU WITH ANYTHING THAT YOU WANT".

I stood up and was amazed and then I heard the voice say again "LIVE BY MY COMMANDMENTS AND I WILL BLESS YOU WITH ANYTHING THAT YOU WANT"! I said is that you LORD?

And then I started praying and meditating on GOD again saying in my mind, "BREATH IN THE HOLY SPIRIT, LET OUT THE DEVIL, BREATH IN THE POSITIVE AND OUT

WITH THE NEGATIVE" and I repeated that over again until I blacked out and fell on my face.

I had passed out and I saw a light the color of the sun, and an arm with a robe came across that light and I saw the hand of GOD as it reached out and touched me. I felt that hand of GOD touch me and I awoke instantly.

I opened my eyes and I was trembling and shaken. I felt the presence of the HOLY SPIRIT UPON ME! I then started crying like a baby as my life was flashing before my eyes. I continued to talk to GOD until class started and when I left out of my cell to go to class everyone said that I was glowing.

Later that day I got an attorney visit and he told me that he had worked out a plea deal with the district attorney that would give me 4 years of prison followed by 2 years of probation and that it would run concurrent with all of the other charges from the other three counties. I asked him if I could give him an answer in a couple of days after I pray on it and he said ok.

Later that night I went back to my jail cell and I started talking to GOD and asking HIM to change me and let me know what to do. I spoke to GOD and said to HIM that I'm going away for a long time and I need you to be with me LORD.

I need you to walk this walk with me LORD and be with me when I get out of incarceration LORD. I asked the LORD to clean up my back yard, meaning my past life and to create a new life for me.

That evening when I went to bed I was feeling like I didn't want to live if GOD wasn't going to be in my life so as I lay in my bunk, I spoke to GOD again and told HIM that if HE wasn't going to be in my life and allow me to work for HIM for the rest of my life then to take me in my sleep.

Now I didn't want to kill myself but I wanted GOD to take me in my sleep if HE wasn't going to be with me. I fell asleep and I started dreaming that hundreds of demons were trying to kill me.

They looked like ninja demons coming up from below or beneath me and they had swords and were trying to kill me. As they sliced at me I had a sword and I was slicing them and killing them.

There were hundreds of them, and it seemed like the dream would never stop. The dream seemed like it lasted for hours and when I finally killed the last demon and awakened, I was drenched in sweat, and totally exhausted.

I felt like I couldn't breathe and like there wasn't any air in that tiny jail cell that I was in. I was looking at the ceiling, exhausted and thinking about what I had just dreamed and all of a sudden while my eyes were opened, a demon came from out of what seemed to be nowhere! It was bigger than all the rest to them and it tried to stab me in my heart.

I put my left hand over my heart just in time and the point of the demons sword hit my hand but didn't penetrate it. I had a sword in my hand and I sliced that demon in half and all of a sudden I was fully awake.

I was still soaked and wet with sweat like I had been in a real battle but I could breathe now. I felt serenity, calm and peaceful like a new spirit of life had come upon me. It was more than just a dream and the demons that plagued me all of my life where cast out of me that evening.

That day when I got up and went to study I felt rejuvenated and filled with vigor, ambition, and motivation to serve GOD with true surrender and submission. It was a Wednesday and we had bible class all day long.

One of the instructors didn't show up and I got the opportunity to preach and teach class that day. Every Wednesday evening we have chapel and that evening there were some outside ministers that came in to preach and teach.

There were 73 men in the chapel that evening and I was sitting with my elbows on my knees praying to GOD. As I asked GOD what should I do in reference to the plea deal that was offered to me of 4 years of prison time, I felt the presence of the LORD upon me again.

I felt the LORDS hand on my shoulder as if to comfort me. I opened my eyes and I saw two legs and feet standing there. They were in sandals and had a ashy look.

There was a robe that came down below the knee and just above the ankles and I tried to look up but I couldn't. I was so overwhelmed that I started crying again and I heard the voice of the LORD say to me that "THIS IS YOUR LAST CHAPTER"! I Spoke back to the LORD and said, what do you mean by my last chapter LORD? I was crying and talking to the LORD out loud in front of 73 thugs in jail.

Everyone already had got to know me as Reverend Og Willie J, and they knew that I wasn't a punk or anyone to mess with. I could hold my own and worked hard on my Mind, Body, and Spirit!

But never the less the presence of the LORD broke me down to weep like a baby. So I was talking to the LORD and asking HIM what HE meant by "This Was My Last Chapter" and I heard the LORD say that HE has cleared the path of my life.

He said that HE was going to send me home and that I had to save my children, and be a beacon of light to all that

I encounter. I continued crying and having my conversation with the LORD. I saw JESUS CHRIST walk with me up to the judge in the court room and walk with me out of the court house, and HE was walking with me down a clear, narrow, path of life.

When my conversation and vision was over with the LORD, everyone including the Pastor and outside visiting ministers were standing around me and we all prayed together. I told them that "JESUS CHRIST was just there and that the HOLY SPIRIT was with us right now". Everyone was amazed and we all rejoiced at that moment.

The next day my attorney came to visit me to have me sign the documents to agree to the plea bargain that they offered me. I told him that GOD told me that HE was going to send me home so I wasn't going to sign any of those documents.

My lawyer said to me Mr Wiggins, you signed a confession and they also recorded your confession so they are not going to let you off. He said that if I go to trial with this that I was looking at a minimum of 20 years and a maximum of 40 years in prison.

He said "Mr. Wiggins, it's alright that you believe in GOD but if you don't sign this plea bargain you are going to go away for a very long time. I stated again to him that GOD said that HE was going to send me home.

He told me that because of the fact that I wouldn't sign the plea deal that he would have to reschedule another court date for me which would be in 60 more days. He left very disappointed and I went back to my cell to continue what I was doing.

I had already started writing this book; my life story but when GOD came upon me that day in the chapel and I heard the voice of the LORD tell me that this was my last chapter, HE put it upon my heart to write my first book that is in stores titled "THE LAST CHAPTER".

I just wanted to help those who were and is walking in the shadow of darkness to find their way to the light of JESUS CHRIST! At first my family didn't know that I was in jail and I had no way of contacting them.

My girl friend Theresa was my only outside contact at that time. I didn't want to ask her for any money because we had gotten a beautiful home together and I knew that she would have to hold things down while I was locked up.

To write I would get paper out of the trash and use whatever documents and paper that I had or could find. I could remember writing and piecing together the book The Last Chapter. I would sit up for the woo hours of the night until I couldn't keep my eyes open anymore.

I would be so tired that I would find myself writing and looking up at the ceiling or at the walls while falling asleep. One day about three weeks into writing The Last Chapter I didn't even know what I had written and I never stopped to think about that.

So I got all of my papers together and organized, and I started reading what I had written. I said to myself, "I wrote this!" It was truly amazing to me that I had written such profound words.

I would never have ever thought that I would be a professional author never mind a man of GOD! Well the time came for me to go to court, and I was brought into the court room, and as I stood up my lawyer told the judge that I refuse to accept the plea bargain.

The judge asked me if I was under the influence of any drugs or was I convinced by anyone not to take the plea bargain. I said no and he stated "Mr. Wiggins, you know that you signed a confession and that if you go to trial with this than you would surely lose.

He reminded me that I was looking at a minimum of 20 years and a maximum of 40 years in prison. I asked the judge if I could address the court and I started telling him about how I heard the voice of the LORD and how I saw him.

I told him how the LORD came upon me and how the LORD told me to save my children, my family, and told me that I was going to write a book called "The Last Chapter" and everyone in the court started laughing, even the district attorney and my lawyer were laughing.

Once again a miracle happened, the judge looked at me and said that he was going to drop my charges. He said that he was going to let me go but that I had a hold on me from the other counties that had charges on me.

So I would have to wait until they came to pick me up. Everyone in the court was amazed and my lawyer was amazed that my charges was dropped. As I was being escorted out of the court room I looked at my lawyer and said

"I told you that GOD told me that he was going to set me free". They had my confession on paper and on a recording and my charges were dropped! That was an act of GOD! Several days later the Lee county jail came to get me and brought me to the Lee county jail.

That jail is the second dirtiest, roughest, and toughest jail in Florida. Miami Dade county jail is the first. I was processed into the jail and brought to the holding tank which is where everyone who is arrested and booked into that jail is put.

It must have been about one hundred inmates in that holding tank, all of whom were of different gangs, and ethnic races. There were rats and roaches crawling around, and everyone was either on edge or wanted to show forth their manhood (power).

I instantly went into each section of the tank and observed to see who was controlling that section. One of the things that happen in any jail are fights over the control over the telephones.

There are only two or three phones at the most in every holding tank in every jail that I have ever been in. In the holding tank everyone sleeps were ever they can. You are giving mats to sleep on, and you have to find a spot to put it.

It smells of 100 men who haven't showered or bathed, and everyone sleeps right next to one another. I was sitting on my mat reading my pocket bible that the guards allowed me to bring into the holding tank with me and a young man who was 26 years of age asked me if I could say a prayer for him.

I said a prayer for him that GOD be graceful and merciful on him for whatever he was there for. He then started telling me how he got arrested for selling weed on the campus of the college that he went to.

He was a star running back for Florida State University and now that he was arrested he feared that he would lose his scholarship. He also told me that he got his girlfriend pregnant, and they had a baby boy.

That was why he started selling weed so that he would have money to support his child. He asked me to pray for him and I did. After the prayer we talked about how he had to eliminate the negative people, places and things out of his life in order to succeed on a positive path.

I told him how I lived mine life in the past and how the Holy Ghost came upon me and GOD had saved me! As I was telling him of my sins, criminal past, and of how GOD had cleared the path of my life and told me that HE was going to send me home, he started asking me several questions about GOD.

I answered him as if speaking the very words of GOD, quoting Bible verses, preaching and teaching him. Then several other inmates asked if they could sit with us and listen.

A couple of more of them asked if I could bless them with a prayer and before I knew it 16 guys had joined in and sat with us and discussed the Bible and the Christian way of life. After two days I was taken to what they call the stockade.

It looked like dungeons or zoo cages with a little door that led to a room that was suppose to hold 30 men but there were 117 men in placed in there. It was so overcrowded that I saw two different fights over inmates trying to claim a sleeping spot.

I however walked right to a spot and claimed it and no one said a thing to me. I instantly started working out and then took a cold shower because there wasn't any hot water. I then went to my sleeping spot to read my Bible, closed my eyes and said a prayer.

Once again as I did at the Sarasota jail I would get up early in the morning, pray and meditate on GOD and study the Holy Bible. The stockade was the roughest and toughest unit of the Lee County jail and Once again I was tested by the thugs to see if I was a punk but of course Og Willie J put them in their place and once again the strong preyed on the weak.

It wasn't long before I gained the respect of the inmates there and they were coming to me for prayer and advice. There was a guy name Zeke and one named Dread who were running our cage.

One morning before breakfast I was sitting in the dinning part our cage were we eat at reading my Bible and Zeke was on the phone with his girlfriend. He was yelling at her, cussing and fussing on the phone and then all of a sudden he slammed the phone down and broke it.

He walked away from the phone furious with a look of death in his eyes and as he walked passed my table I said to him, "Zeke you want your life back"? He told me to mind my business and I said to him you can have you girl and your life back Zeke.

He walked up to the table where I was sitting and said "I told you too mind your fucking business Rev, now say something else!" I said "FATHER GOD" as I grabbed Zeke's wrist and started praying for him. As I was praying I started speaking in tongues in a commanding voice and Zeke fell backwards and busted his head on the concrete floor and was knocked out cold.

I opened my eyes from the prayer and kneeled down beside him and he opened his eyes and started crying and shouting out loud "you're an angel man, GOD sent you hear to me!" I heard Dread say what fuck was that and I looked back at Dread and said come and get some of this Dread! He yelled at me saying "you are not going to do any of that voodoo shit on me!" I said "this isn't any voodoo shit, it's the Holy Spirit of GOD!"

Zeke got up and went to his bed and he couldn't stop crying. From that day forward, everyone looked at me as a man of GOD. They knew that the spirit of GOD was upon me and every day before each meal I would stand up and bless our food.

Every night before bed, I would give short teachings and pray with the men before we went to sleep. We went from being the roughest and toughest unit there to being the cleanest, relaxed and respected unit.

After two months there in the dungeon I was called for an attorney visit in which my attorney told me that he got me a plea bargain for four years of prison followed by two years of probation. That was the same deal that they offered me at the Sarasota County jail. I refused to accept that deal and I refused to accept this one also.

I knew that GOD was with me and that GOD was going to send me home. My lawyer told me that I would be there for another month or two waiting to go before the judge because I didn't take the plea bargain.

He then told me about the GOD Pod that they had their in the Lee County jail which was suppose to be better than the one at the Sarasota County jail so I put in my application to be sent there and it was approved in two days.

On the day when the guards came into the cage at the stockade and told me to pack it up for the GOD Pod, at least 10 inmates came \up to me and told me how I had impacted their lives while I was there with them.

As I got my belongings together Dread said to me, "I guess your job is done here, it's time for you to leave your flock." I didn't see it like that until a couple of weeks later in the GOD Pod. Once I got to that GOD Pod, they invited me to be on the spiritual council within one week.

I continued on seeking GOD diligently, and praying without ceasing. I told of how GOD came upon me at the

Sarasota jail and of the spiritual gifts that GOD had bestowed upon me. I also gave testimony to how GOD had spoken to me several times and how I saw the LORD JESUS CHRIST! Pastor Klamp was the head of the GOD Pod and he was there the night that I spoke and gave testimony as to how GOD spoke to me and how I saw the LORD JESUS CHRIST.

Pastor Klamp said to me out loud, in front of everyone that was there that night, that I didn't hear GOD'S voice because GOD doesn't speak to us in that way anymore and then Pastor Klamp said that I didn't see JESUS CHRIST either. He said that I was imagining, but I stated back to him that if I was hallucinating or hearing things than I want to hear some more of that and to see GOD some more!

If I was hallucinating then that was some good hallucinations and I want more! I learned a lot there at the GOD Pod and became more intimate with the LORD! I was offered the same plea bargain deal there that I was offered at the Sarasota county jail and I refused to take that offer and when I went to court my charges was dropped once again and once again the district attorney and other attorneys were shocked and amazed.

When I was released from the Lee county jail I was brought to the Charlotte County jail in which the LORD continued to use me as a vessel in touching upon other inmates lives. I was released from there on one year house arrest followed by two years of probation.

While I was incarcerated for that year I experienced things that most men of GOD have never experienced in their life time. A young lady (my girlfriend) by the name of Theresa Soto was the only person who was there for me at that time and I shared with her my experiences as they happened.

She was the one person who was there for me when I got out of jail, and the very next day she brought me to a church that she had been going to in North Port Florida. Theresa Aka Terry is a beautiful Italian Christian woman who didn't understand quite yet the anointing of the HOLY SPIRIT upon a person and how the HOLY SPIRIT empowered me.

When we got to the church that she was attending I felt that it was a very spirited church and I got up and walked to the front of the church where people was on their knees praying at the altar. The Pastor and his assistant of that church was on their knees at their chairs on the stage praying and I walked up to the front of the church, and stood there as I felt the power of the HOLY SPIRIT over flowing in abundance in me. My hands were shaken out of control and all of a sudden I felt like I was in another dimension.

CHAPTER 11

A Vessel; Power of the Holy Spirit

All of a sudden I couldn't see anyone in the church except a woman who was kneeling down at the altar praying. There were at least 200 people in the church and I could hear them crying and I could hear their pleas for mercy and call to JESUS CHRIST.

It was like I was in their minds because I heard their cries of pain and torment. I had asked Terry to come with me up to the front of the church but she didn't so I walked up to the woman whom the Holy Spirit led me too and I told her that the LORD was here and wants me to pray for her.

I asked her if I could pray for her and she nodded her head yes. The Holy Spirit was overflowing in me so much that my hands were still shaken, and I placed my hand on her head but I couldn't stop my hand from shaken.

It was shaken so bad that I was hitting her on the head so I slid my hand down to her neck and I was finally able to get control of the shaken. I started praying upon her and speaking in tongues as my voice got louder and louder.

The woman then screamed and passed out. I laid her down and asked a couple of women to stay with her. As the woman screamed and I was laying her down, The pastor of that church who was on the stage kneeling in prayer at his chair, lifted his head and his eyes met my eyes and he had a look of disgust on his face that I have never forgot.

He stood up and walked off of the stage and out of the church and went into his office. I continued moving as a vessel of the LORD in the church by laying hands on people and praying upon them.

They were passing out and others were crying and coming up to me saying "Praise you brother," but I would say back to them "don't praise me, praise JESUS CHRIST, I'm just a vessel". When it was all done the assistant pastor came up to me and said to me that "it was a blessing to have me there".

Terry had come up to the front of the church and was crying also. I took her by the hand and led her towards the door as many more people was acknowledging what they had just witnessed.

Before I could walk out of the door the assistant pastor came up to me and said that the pastor wanted to meet me and talk to me. He was smiling and told me that "GODS favor was upon me and it was a honor for me to be there".

I walked with him into the pastor's office he the pastor had the same look of disgust on his face that he had when his eyes met my eyes at the altar. His arms where folded and he said to me "I don't know what form of ministry this is but you will never come back into my church and do this again".

At that time the anointing that had GOD had given me was all new to me but I knew that it was from GOD and was a privilege and an honor to be used by GOD in this way. I told him that I did nothing but just what GOD wanted me to do and I started telling him how GOD came upon me in jail.

He got angry and said to me "YOU WERE IN JAIL, I DON'T WANT TO TALK TO YOU" and then he told his assistant to talk to me. His assistant who was the man who stayed in the church.

He didn't walk out like the pastor, but whom witnessed the power of the HOLY SPIRIT working through me, then shunned me and said the same thing as his pastor "You was in jail, I don't want to talk to you!"

I was hurt emotionally by their actions and I never returned to that church. I did however go to other churches and I continued to lay hands upon people whenever the pastor of a church would call people to the altar.

I encountered similar attitudes and rejection, but there were a few that really embraced me, and accepted me as a vessel of the LORD, GOD, JESUS CHRIST! I made friends with some pastors and ministers that invited me to their churches.

While I was in the GOD Pod in jail I had studied and memorized a great deal of the verses in the bible so I could quote them and whenever I would speak to other ministers and pastors I would speak the very words of GOD.

One day I was on the bus and my daughter called me on the telephone from Boston and asked me to pray for her. I prayed out loud on that bus and other people heard me and asked me to pray for them.

I started praying for each of them right there on the bus and the bus driver told me that he was a minister and would like to talk to me so we exchanged phone numbers. We became friends and he invited me to come to his church.

I went there and was asked to come back and give testimony of my salvation. I did and I held a revival that afternoon, as I anointed everyone in the church. GOD used me as a vessel in the laying on of hands upon some in healing, and some in spiritual deliverance.

134

When the church service was over with, people were coming up to me saying that they was going to come to my church when I opened it. They said this in front of the pastor of that church and he just walked away and went into the back room. I never meant for this to happen, I was only making myself available as a vessel to the LORD.

I called the pastor who had become my friend and invited me there and he wouldn't answer the phone. Finally I ran into him one day and I asked him why he wouldn't return my calls and he said that he was very busy.

As we continued to talk he said to me that I didn't impress him with all that quoting of the Holy Bible. I told him that I wasn't trying to impress him but as in 1 Peter 4:11 states "if anyone speaks he should do it as one speaking the very words of GOD".

I went on to walk into other churches as a vessel of GOD and was called back to some to preach and teach the word of GOD and to some to demonstrate the power of the HOLY SPIRIT. I have been told to not come back to some churches in which I gladly have not because I know that my job was done there and GOD had used me as he ordained.

I have been told that everything is done in decency and in order and that I shouldn't just walk into another man church and do that. Well there is nothing out of order about the HOLY SPIRIT and everything is decent about the HOLY SPIRIT.

Also we should never quench the HOLY SPIRIT. I know now also that I am not here as a vessel to announce that I am coming to your church but to come to it in humble submission to the will of GOD.

You will not know at what time I may show up at your church, but you will know me by the presence of the LORD upon me. During the first year of being released from jail I finished writing the book "The Last Chapter" and submitted it to several publishing companies.

I was still on house arrest but they didn't put a bracelet on me and allowed me to continue going to churches and organizations to preach and teach the word of GOD. That year was a hard year for me because I had no job and the economy was starting to get bad.

I enrolled in school at Kaplan University online and went to a daily labor hall for work. I would get up at 3am every morning and ride a bicycle for one hour to the labor work force and wait to be called out for work.

I didn't get called out for three weeks but I never stopped going and waiting on the LORD to give me work. I worked in the hot sun of 95 degrees of heat doing hard labor for $7.00 an hour, 8 to 10 hours a day.

When I was finished with work I would go back to the labor hall and get my check every day and then ride my bike to cash the check and ride it for one hour back home. I remember praying to GOD to help me to make it back home because I was so tired.

I would be exhausted by the time I got home, and then I had school work to do. I prayed and prayed for the LORD to exalt me. I had moved in with Terry when I got out of jail and things weren't going so well with her and I.

We had a lot of differences and disagreements that brought us a lot of pain and suffering in our relationship. I found myself able to help everyone else with their relationships but I wasn't able to correct the problems with my own relationship with Terry.

I will reveal the nature of these problems which will also be discussed in my next book that will be titled "Intimacy". Sometimes I would get only a few hours of sleep and things were up and down with Terry and I.

I went into deep, deep prayer and meditation as I sought comfort in the LORD and in HIS mighty power. Then I released my problems into the hands of GOD, and HE soon worked it all out for me.

I started taking showers and oiling myself down with lotions and consecrated oil that I prayed upon and then laying a blanket on the floor of my bedroom and laying there talking to GOD.

HE would always talk back to me and reveal things to me. HE told me when Terry was going to get sick and when things were going to happen at her job and school that she was attending.

He told me of money that I was going to receive that I did in fact receive. One day in a vision, I saw my landlord chasing his wife and throwing the Bible at her. She was dragging her children along and was dressed up to go to church.

She got into her white van and I followed her. She drove to a brick building in which is where her church was at and she went in as I got out of my car and followed her.

It was upstairs on the second floor and there where people of different nationalities there. The white people were sitting together and sat very quietly with no expressions on their face at all, and were wearing nice clothing.

The black people all sat together and had sad looks upon their face's, they looked poor and were quiet. The Spanish people were all sitting together and laughing out loud as if they didn't have a care in the world.

There were people walking around in \the church. I saw an old man walk pass me with a cane, a child run pass me, and there were children jumping rope in there. It was very hectic. Now remember this is a vision that I had awaken too. I started walking around in the church and speaking in tongues as I prayed to GOD.

I came to a big window that overlooked the world and I looked out of the window and saw explosions, earthquakes, title waves, and war. All of a sudden the LORD JESUS CHRIST came in from that window and stood in front of me.

HE looked around in the church and then looked at me and started crying. HIS eyes opened up and let me into his soul. I felt his love for us, and then his pain and suffering, and all that HE was feeling at that time.

I started crying uncontrollably as I found myself standing there looking into the eyes of JESUS CHRIST! I will never forget that moment! When the LORD made his exit, and the vision was over, I couldn't stop crying and feeling his emotions of LOVE for us, and pain and suffering.

What I had been through in life was nothing compared to what JESUS CHRIST endured and suffered for us! I still cry sometimes to this day when I think of it but I know that It is a great blessing, honor and privilege to have seen the LORD!

Customers & Supporters at various Book Signings

I have traveled the country doing book signings and speaker engagements as a motivational speaker, preacher and man of GOD, as a result of writing that book, and this book that you are reading now is my second book that I have written.

I will established the Strong Roots Church of JESUS CHRIST this year and on I am currently working on a inspirational gospel CD in which I plan to have released in 2012 and I will continue to make myself available to the LORD to use me as HE ordains.

CHAPTER 12

Letters to my Family!

From: Minister Willie Wiggins Jr   July 11, 2009

Peace & Blessings to you my beloved mother and father, children, brothers, sisters, aunts, uncles, nieces, nephew and cousins. I love you all!I am writing this letter to you, and will send out a letter, with my personnel prayer blessing on it to you, each and every month.

I pray that the peace and blessings of God come upon you and your family. I want you to know that God loves you and will never leave you. You may step away from God sometimes by not abiding in his laws, (commandments), but he will always be there waiting on your return. God loves you unconditionally.

Love is God's greatest attribute and if we want to have just a fraction of God's qualities, and character in us then we should start by forgiving one another for all that we have ever done to each other and love one another as God loves us.

The Bible says in 1 John 4:7 Beloved, let us love one another, for love is of God, and everyone who loves is born of God, and knows God. I love you and miss you, and I think of you often. I include you and your family in my prayers everyday faithfully.

As I continue to make myself available to the Lord so that he may continue to use me to help other, I'm thinking of how I can help you. I know that I can help you with my prayers, and with the word of God, and in spirit, truth, encouragement and love!

God continues to strengthen me and allow me to become more intimate with him. My spiritual growth has allowed me to get closer to God then I ever could have imagined. He continues to touch his hand upon me in some very special ways that I will tell you about later.

I am going to Pray now and type the prayer here on this letter. After I type it on this letter I will hold it to my heart and pray upon it again, so that as God has touched his hand upon me, he will touch his hand upon you that you may receive the anointing of the Holy Spirit upon you in due time (if you haven't already received the Holy Spirit).

For my dear family members that do not know, the Holy Spirit is the Spirit of God. So as God has touched upon me, I touch upon you with this prayer, presented in the name of my Lord and savior Jesus Christ.

I pray this upon you and your family. Dear heavenly father, God of all Gods, father of all fathers, in the name of Jesus Christ our Lord and savior, I ask you father God that you touch your might hand upon my family member here.

As a father does, he watches over his children, provide for them, comfort them, teach them and guide them to the right path of life. As our father, God, I am asking that you provide food, clothing and shelter upon us all always.

Father God, for my family members that do not understand you, and the Christian way of life, I am asking you father God to boldly open up their heart that they may lend me their hear as I bring to them the word of life, your word father. I pray father God with love and respect that they hear me and receive this prayer.

I ask that you comfort them when they are feeling down, protect them in all that they do, and let your mercy, grace and favor be upon them father God. Strengthen them mentally, physically, spiritually, and financially father God.

And these things I pray to you from my heart father God in the name of Jesus Christ. AMEN !!!I love you all once again and will see you all very soon. **Romans 15:13** May the God of hope, fill you with all joy and peace as you trust in him, so that you my over flow with hope by the power of the Holy Spirit.

Minister Willie Wiggins Jr (aka Reverend OG Willie J)

September, 3rd 2009

Minister Willie Wiggins Jr

With Love I write this month's letter.

We recently lost a family member to cancer; our cousin Jimmy in New York. My prayers go out to our family there, and those who were closest to him. I know that he is in a better place, living in the spirit of God, in spirit, as opposed to living here on earth in the flesh.

We as a family are so lost, we are so divided and out of contact with each other. This is why we are weak as a family, as a unit and as a member (part) of the body of Christ. Satan is surely doing his job which is to divide and conquer us.

He wants to destroy us anyway that he can. Satan knows everything about you; you're weaknesses, your strengths, and your desires. He put hate, vain glory, envy, and jealousy in your hearts, mind and soul.

143

He breaks up marriages, father from son, daughter from mother, aunts, uncles, cousins and grandparents and all of us from each other. He creates selfish desires in your hearts and minds, and causes you to not look out for each other, to not be there for each other.

Some of our family members are totally caught up in Satan's web, selling drugs, doing drugs, fornicating, committing adultery, lying, stealing, and so much more. Am I my brother's keeper?

Yes I am, and that is why every month, I will send these letters in hope that it may help one of you. One of my jobs as a Minister of God is to bring the light of Jesus Christ to you. If you are already a Christian, then you are a torch bearer, one who overcomes, and you are your brother and sister's keeper.

As Christians we are one in spirit; this means that the same spirit that is leading me is the same spirit that is leading you, (the Holy Spirit) the spirit of Jesus Christ! You are conforming to become Christ like right. Well why aren't you reaching out to help your family?

How come you're not making yourselves available to each other? Why won't you pick up the phone and greet one another or send an email or letter? Why is it that we only see each other and tell each other how much we love each other, when someone in the family passes away!

Don't let Satan keep our family apart. Don't let him make you feel weak or like you don't have time for each other because you have to watch your favorite television show or you got something better to do then doing the work of God as a Christian man or woman.

We are family, and children of God, and I want each and every one of you that reads this letter, to pick up the phone and call someone in the family that you haven't heard from in a long time, and tell them that you love them.

Find out what is going on with them and how we may help them as a family. If they are failing in life, we need to at least attempt to help them. If they are sick or failing in health then let us all contact one another and set a time for prayer everyday at the same time that we will pray for them until they are well.

James 5:16 Confess your faults one to another, and pray one for another, that you may be healed. The effectual fervent prayer of a righteous man availeth much. If someone is in desperate financial need then let's all put $1 to $5 each in a fund to help them, it's not a lot of money but I know that it will help them and uplift them.

I have each of your addresses but I don't have your phone numbers, please send me your phone numbers by phone 941-623-7897 or email strongrootschurchofchrist@gmail.com **James 4:14** You do not know what will happen tomorrow, for what is your life? It is even a vapor that appears for a little time and then vanishes away.

1 John 4:7 Beloved, let us love one another, for love is of God, and everyone who loves is born of God, and knows God.

Prayer

In the name of Jesus Christ I give thanks to God for all things and matters of life, for I know father God, that you are the propitiation of all of our lives. I ask you father God in the name of Jesus Christ that you conciliate our family and give us your strength father God, so that we will walk in the light of Jesus Christ always reaching out to help others, starting with our own family.

We are approaching flew season father God and Satan has planted another virus (the swine flu) upon us. Dear Lord Jesus,

I know that you are walking this earth. I ask you Lord Jesus and our father in heaven to eradicate Satan and the diseases that he brings about.

Keep all cold, flu, sickness, illness and disease from coming down on us Father God in the name of Jesus Christ. Amen!

10/07/09

October Family letter

Peace & Blessings to you all and with love I write to you this month.

This month's letter is about love and respect in relationships, between each and every one of you as a family member, friend, girlfriend, boyfriend or husband and wife.

Love is Gods most powerful attribute! Jesus said in the book of Matthew and Mark the greatest commandment is **Mark 12:30** love the lord your God with all your heart, and with all your soul and with all mind and with all your strength. We are to love God first above all things, and then learn to love ourselves and one another as our neighbors.

1 John 4:7 Beloved, let us love one another, for love is of God, and everyone who loves is born of God and knows God.

John 13:34 A new commandment I give unto you, that ye love one another; as I have loved you, that ye also love one another.

People yearn of love all their lives. Lives are destroyed because of broken relationships and children growing up

146

without loving parents and without the act of love being shown and expressed in their lives.

So what they experience is hate and anger. If you don't show your love and act it out towards your children, companion and one another then you are not giving your love to them.

You're holding it in, and keeping it to yourself. Don't be afraid to hug and kiss one another and tell each other that you love them. Letting someone know that you love them goes deep into the very core and essence of a person's heart and is a healing emotion.

It will lift you up when you're feeling down. The Bible says Love is patient, Love is kind, it does not envy, it does not boast, it is not proud. It is not rude, it is not self seeking, and it is not easily angered.

It keeps no record of wrongs; love does not delight in evil but rejoices with the truth. It always protects, always trusts, always hopes, and always perseveres. Love never fails. I bring the word of God to you about love, in hope that you understand the importance of it in life and in your relationship with God and each other.

Family, show your love to one another. Once again, pick up the phone and call someone who you haven't talked to in a long time and tell them that you love them. Stop walking around harboring envies, jealousy, and hate towards one another. Stop judging one another, thinking that you're better than one or another. Remember that everyone has the power to change and I know that from my own experiences.

Now all of you who have a companion or a spouse read this together. This is what the Bible says about Marriage and since some of you aren't married, you can apply this to your relationship with your companion.

The sacred, covenantal union of one man and one woman formed when the two swear before God an oath of lifelong loyalty and love to each other. God instituted the first marriage in the Garden of Eden when He gave Eve to Adam as his wife Gen 2:18-25.

That later marriages were to follow the pattern of the first is indicated by the concluding divine instruction. Go to Matthew 19:4-6 in the Bible; this is why a man leaves his father and mother and bonds with his wife, and they become one in the flesh. The oneness of marriage separated the couple from others as a distinct family unit.

Marriage is also God's unique gift to provide the framework for intimate companionship, as a means for procreation of the human race, and as the channel of sexual expression *according to biblical standards.* The Bible describes the marriage that pleases God in terms of mutual submission empowered by the Holy Spirit (Eph.5:18-21).

The husband is to practice self denying, nurturing love patterned after that of Christ, (Eph 5:25-33). He is the initiator and is responsible for leading his wife with wisdom and understanding.

He is also to protect, provide for and honor her (Col. 3:19). A wife on the other hand, is to express her submission

148

by following her husband's leadership with respect (Eph.5:22-24-33), maintaining a pure and reverent life with a gentle and quiet spirit (1 peter.3:1-6).

My family; stop all of the arguing, fussing and cussing. Be careful what you say out of your mouth, for you can give Satan the right to declare war on you and the rest of our family by what you say.

Now ladies don't get upset but listen carefully. God is the head of Jesus Christ, Christ is the head of man and man is the head of the woman. Not that man should walk around thinking that he can control his woman's life or dominate her.

Not that he should belittle her or talk down at her but that they uphold Gods law. A good woman will automatically give that honor to her husband as her place in the natural order of things and a good man will bestow that honor back upon her. There is no love, like the love of God. **John 3:16** For God so loved the world that he gave his one and only begotten son that who so ever should believe in him should not parish but have eternal life. I love you all; call me anytime at 941-623-7897

Finally, my book "THE LAST CHAPTER" by Minister Willie Wiggins Jr Aka Reverend OG Willie J. is available now online at PublishAmerica.com or call 301-695-1707 they may ask for the ISBN# 978-1-4489-2191-1

Prayer

I pray that the will of God be done upon each and every one of us and that we live according to his will. I pray that God continues to be graceful to us, bless us and make his face shine upon us that our ways be known on earth and our salvation upon nations.

I pray that the curse of Satan that has plagued our family for many years be lifted up off of us by the power of the Father, the Son and the Holy Spirit, and that God blesses us with the best of health, wealth, knowledge, wisdom and understanding. Amen!

November 08, 2009

Family Letter
Minister Willie Wiggins Jr
A Visit From Satan!!

Satan is calling you and wants to take possession or your life, and to possess your heart, mind body, and soul. Believe it or not, Satan visits you every day. This is how he does it!!Hello my friend, my name is Satan, I've come to visit you once again.

I love to see you suffer mentally, physically, spiritually, financially and socially. I want to make you restless so you can never relax. I want you to be jumpy, nervous and anxious. I want to make you agitated and irritable, so everything and everybody makes you uncomfortable.

I want you to be confused and depressed so that you can't think clearly or positively. I want you to feel guilty and remorseful for the things you have done in the past that you will never be able to let go of it. I want to make you angry and hateful toward the world for the way it is and the way you are.

I want you to feel sorry for yourself and blame everything but your drug and alcohol use for the way things is. I want you to be deceitful and untrustworthy and to manipulate and con as many people as possible. I want to make you fearful and paranoid for no reason at all. I want you to wake up during all hours of the night and scream for me. You know you can't sleep without me.

I'm even in your dreams. I want to be the first thing you wake up to every morning, and the last thing you touch before you black out. I would rather kill you, but I'll be happy enough to put you back in the hospital, another institution or jail. But you know I'll be waiting for you when you get out. I love to watch you slowly going insane.

I love to see the physical damage I'm causing you. I can't help but sneer and chuckle when you shiver and shake, when you freeze and sweat at the same time, and when you wake with your sheets and blankets soaking wet.

It's amusing to watch you make love to the toilet bowl, heaving and watching and not able to hold me down. It's amazing how much destruction I can do to your internal organs while at the same time work on your brain!

Think about this family, this is what Satan has planned for us from the time we were born. Our only protection against Satan is our father God Almighty, and the way to the father is through the son, Jesus Christ!! Now let's pray and rebuke Satan together.

Upon receiving this letter, call me and I will pray with you to rebuke Satan, by the power of God, In the name of Jesus Christ by the demonstration of the power of the Holy Spirit! My phone# is 941-623-7897 For those of you who can't call me or won't call me, I pray in the name of Jesus Christ, by the blood of Jesus Christ and the power of our father God almighty that you receive the blessing of the holy spirit as we rebuke Satan all together and bind him and his demons together and cast them back to where they came from in the name of Jesus Christ, by the blood of Jesus Christ, praise God, AMEN!!

Don't forget my book "The Last Chapter" we be in stores on Saturday, November 14. Always give them the ISBN# 978-1-4489-2191-1 when you ask for it at a store.

IT IS AVAILABLE FOR ORDER NOW THOUGH!

ORDER DIRECT ONLINE AT PUBLISHAMERICA.COM OR BY PHONE 301-695-1707 RECEIVE IT IN TWO DAYS DELIVERY.

IT WILL ALSO BE IN STORES NATION WIDE, ON NOVEMBER

14, 2009 GIVE ISBN # 978-1-4489-2191-1

ORDER YOURS NOW!! It will change your life forever!

For more information go to:

PublishedAuthors.net/MinisterWillieWigginsJr/index/html

December, 2009

From Minister Willie Wiggins Jr

Grace and much peace be multiplied unto you. I pray that you are well. I would like to share a few words of Love with you and also share a song with you. The song is on love:

http://www.youtube.com/watch?v=_qaVwnkhsvU   And the words of Love are these:

John 15: 9 "As the Father has loved me, so have I loved you. Now remain in my love. 10 If you obey my commands, you will remain in my love, just as I have obeyed my Father's commands and remain in his love. 11 I have told you this so that my joy may be in you and that your joy may be complete. 12 My command is this: Love each other as I have loved you. 13 Greater love has no one than this, that he lay down his life for his friends. 14You are my friends if you do what I command. 15 I no longer call you servants, because a servant does not know his master's business. Instead, I have called you friends, for everything that I learned from my Father I have made known to you. 16 You did not choose me, but I chose you and appointed you to go and bear fruit? fruit that will last. Then the Father will give you whatever you ask in my name. 17 This is my command: Love each other.Much love to you and all around you Today!

GOD is the conciliator, and propitiator of all things and will restore respect & honor upon you!

Minister Willie Wiggins Jr

Peace and blessings to you my beloved Family.

I just got through a grueling week of finals in school, Praise God!

I have a message for you all from God; He says why should you worry about anything as long as you walk with him?

No one loves you more than he does and no one cares about your life more the he does he said. No one watches over you more then I God said and no one wants a relationship with you more than I do God says.I am God over all your life, your career, your marriage, and your family.

From the time you wake up in the morning to the time you finally rest your head on the pillow at night, I trust that you will feel My presence, God says. I will be with you every step of the way to bring you peace and to give you wisdom, strength, and encouragement.

I know that at times you feel as if you are all alone, but that feeling is further from the truth then you can imagine. As My follower you have a number of examples of My presence in your life. In addition to always being present with you,

I have sent to you the Holy Spirit, who guides, encourages, and comforts you. But there is one more form of My companionship that is often overlooked or taken for granted, the special communion you can have with other believers.

I love to be with you, and I long for you to seek me with all your heart. In fact, I created you so we could be in a relationship with each other. Your Father, your Friend, your God with love! Family,

I know your mind is filled with daily and myriad things that overwhelm you. You have deadlines to meet, budgets to plan, and meetings to attend. You face mortgage payments, family responsibilities, church commitments, and many other things.

You're left wondering whether you will ever be able to breathe easily again. I have one work for you: Come to God. Come to God, you who are burdened and tired, and he will give you rest, and peace, and joy, and happiness.

Don't let others lead you to believe that peace will only come when you are dead, or after you graduate from college, or when you finally land that perfect job, or when the kids move out, or when you strike it rich, or when you retire.

Peace doesn't come from external experiences or because of your plans. True Peace is found in God through Jesus Christ! And he will give it to you abundantly. All you have to do is to ask for it in the name of Jesus Christ and he will give it to you, so come to God and he will come to you.

March 2010

The Lord has called upon me to do a great and mighty job. He has duly and properly prepared me for the task at hand and is continually perfecting me. Psalm

138:8 The Lord will perfect that which concerneth me, thy mercy oh Lord, are works of thy own hands.

The Holy Spirit upon me is continuing to grow and strengthen as I continue to talk to the Lord and he continues to talk back to me. As God has blessed me with gifts of healing, anointing in the laying on of hands, prayer, discernment, prophecy, visions as a see'er, interpretation of tongues, and is continually giving me knowledge, wisdom and understanding, God is going to unleash me upon the world this year.

I thank God for all of his blessings and his presence upon me. I thank God for his presence upon you my beloved family. Psalm 103:24 Bless the Lord, O my soul, and forget not all his benefits: Who forgiveth all thine iniquities; who healeth all thy diseases; who redeemeth thy life from destruction; who crowneth thee with loving kindness and tender mercies.

Jesus said in his word to not worry or have any anxiety about anything. He said to not take any thought or be concerned about any circumstance in your life. We must cast our care, concern, and worry on the Lord. We must continue to put our trust and confidence in God.

God will take care of us, because he loves us. Let us thank God for his presence and peace in our lives. Jesus said not to let our heart be troubled or afraid, but to keep our mind focused on Him, knowing He will never leave or forsake us.

God's word says that the afflictions of the righteous are many but he will deliver them out of them all. We must keep looking to God and not worry or be in fear about the circumstances of our lives. God said that in this world we would have tribulation, but He told us to be of good cheer and rejoice in all things, because He has overcome the world and will help us do the same.

God's Word says not to take any thought about the future; therefore, we must refuse to worry or be anxious concerning ourfuture. Let us put our future in God's hands, and I know that He will take care of us. 1 Peter 5:7 Casting all your care upon him; for he careth for you. God's Word says that all things work together for good to those who love Him.

What Satan has meant for evil, God will turn for good. Let us be free from worry, and have the victory in the great and mighty name of Jesus Christ! Psalm 107:20 He sent his word and healed them, and delivered them from their destruction.

Exodus 23:25 and ye shall serve the Lord you God, and he shall bless thy bread, and thy water: and I will take sickness away from the midst of thee.

Romans 8: 11 But if the Spirit of him that raised up Jesus from the dead dwell in you, he that raised up Christ from the dead shall also quicken your mortal bodies by his Spirit that dwelleth in you.

Peace and love to you all!

April 2010

Peace and blessings to you all,
With love I write this letter to you.

I want to apologize to my beloved Mother, Father, brothers, sisters, aunts, uncles, cousins, nieces and nephews, whom I didn't get to bless with a prayer upon you, while I was in Boston but I assure you that you are included in my prayers every day.

For all of you who come, I will bless you with an anointing of the Holy Spirit by the authority of Jesus Christ that he has given me on Sunday morning April 13th, at 11am here in Florida and it will change your life forever.

As you may or may not know, we are in spiritual warfare everyday against unseen forces, spirits, demons and Satan himself. Satan is the father of all lies and the author of confusion and confliction.

You are constantly fighting among each other and you really don't ever know why. You blame it on the little things of life and hold grudges for long periods of time. It is Satan

157

who ultimately desires that we hate on one another and not get along or love one another.

It is the spiritual wickedness of Satan that is holding back your financial blessings, creating situations upon you that cause you bad health, and keeping you from having peaceful and meaningful relationships. God always want the very best for you.

It is the incubus and succubus spirits that form a relationship with you and cause you to not be able to get along with your companion. These spirits will even rape you in your sleep causing you to have wet dreams.

I tell you the truth; the only way to stop these things from happening is to plead the blood of Jesus Christ upon you. I will tell you more about this later but for now, as a man of GOD and a warrior, soldier of the LORD, I give you this prayer: RECEIVE THIS!!

Heavenly Father God almighty, in your great and mighty name of "I AM" and in the great and mighty name of Jesus Christ, I prepare for battle. Today I claim victory over Satan by putting on the whole armor of GOD!

I ask that you give armor to my family here on earth, my father, mother, brothers and sisters, aunts, uncles, nephews, nieces and cousins. I put on the girdle of truth and ask that they are giving it.

May we all stand strong and firm in the truth of your word Father GOD, so that we will not be a victim of Satan's lies, confusion and conflict. I ask that you dress us with the breastplate of righteousness! May it guard our hearts from evil so we will remain pure and holy, protected under the blood of Jesus Christ.

158

I plead the blood of Jesus Christ upon each and every one of us in the great and mighty name of Jesus Christ. I ask you Heavenly Father GOD Almighty that you give us the shoes of peace, that we may walk in peace forever!

May we stand firm in the Good News of the Gospel, so your Peace will shine through us, and be a light to all we encounter. I ask that you give us the Shield of Faith and make us ready for Satan's fiery darts of Doubt, Denial, and Deceit, so we will not be vulnerable to spiritual defeat.

We put on the helmet of salvation Lord and I ask that you keep our minds focus on you, Father GOD, and on you LORD JESUS, so that Satan will not have a stronghold on our thoughts. We take the sword of the Holy Spirit! May the two-edged sword of your word be ready in my hands so I can expose the tempting words of Satan.

By faith we have become your warriors and have put on the whole armor of you GOD! We are prepared to live this day in spiritual victory as we plead the blood of Jesus Christ upon us and ask that you cover us with the blood of Jesus Christ and create a wall of protection upon us that Satan can't penetrate, In Jesus Christ name we ask you this. AMEN!! NOW RECEIVE THIS AND WHATCH YOUR LIFE AND LUCK CHANGE. Love you all, Minister Willie Wiggins Jr

Blessed are the Righteous
Psalm 1

Blessed is the man that walk not in the counsel of the ungodly, nor stand in the way of sinners, nor sits in the seat of the scornful. But his delight is in the law of the Lord; and in his law doth he meditate day and night.

And he shall be like a tree planted by the rivers of water, that bring forth his fruit in his season; and whatsoever he doeth shall prosper. The ungodly are not so: but are like the chaff which the wind drives away. Therefore the ungodly shall not stand in the judgment, nor sinners in the congregation of the righteous. For the Lord knows the way of the righteous: but the way of the ungodly shall perish.

The Beatitudes
Matthew 5:3-12

Blessed are the poor in spirit: for theirs is the kingdom of heaven. Blessed are they that mourn: for they shall be comforted. Blessed are the meek: for they shall inherit the earth. Blessed are they which do hunger and thirst after righteousness: for they shall be filled.

Blessed are the merciful: for they shall obtain mercy. Blessed are the pure in heart: for they shall see GOD. Blessed are the peacemakers: for they shall be called the children of GOD. Blessed are they which are persecuted for righteousness sake: for theirs is the kingdom of heaven. Blessed are ye, when men shall revile you, and persecute you, and shall say all manner of evil against you falsely, for my sake.

Rejoice, and be exceeding glad: for great is your reward in heaven: for so persecuted they the prophets which were before you.

The Greatest of these is Love
1 Corinthians 13: 1-13

Though I speak with the tongues of men and of angels, and have not love, I am become as sounding brass, or a tinkling cymbal. And though I have the gift of prophecy, and understand all mysteries, and all knowledge: and though I have all faith, so that I could remove mountains, and have not love, I am nothing. And though I bestow all my goods to feed the poor, and though I give my body to be burned, and have not love, it profiteth me nothing.

Love suffereth long, and is kind: love envieth not: Love vaunteth not itself, is not puffed up, Doth not behave itself unseemly, seeketh not her own, is not easily provoked, thinketh no evil: Rejoiceth not in iniquity, but rejoiceth in the truth; Beareth all things, believeth all things, hopeth all things, endureth all things. Love never faileth: but whether there be prophecies, they shall fail; whether there be tongues, they shall cease; whether there be knowledge, it shall vanish away.

For we know in part, and we prophesy in part. But when that which is perfect is come, then that which is in part shall be done away. When I was a child, I spoke as a child, I understood as a child, I though as a child: but when I became a man, I put away childish things. For now we see through a glass, darkly; but then face to face: Now I know in part; but then shall I know even as also I am known. And now abideth faith, hope, and love, these three; but the greatest of these is LOVE!

I LOVE YOU ALL!

DON'T LET SATAN FOOL YOU!!

SATAN WANTS TO DIVIDE, CONQUER AND DESTROY YOU ANYWAY THAT HE CAN!

HE WANTS YOU TO HATE & ENVY ONE ANOTHER!

SO FORGIVE ONE ANOTHER AND PUT AWAY ALL BITTERNESS AND ANGER AND
CLAMOR AND EVIL SPEAKING AND BE KIND TO ONE ANOTHER!
LOVE IS A HEALING EMOTION AND WILL KEEP YOU FROM BEING SICK!

LOVE!

CPSIA information can be obtained at www.ICGtesting.com
Printed in the USA
LVOW070718261011

252064LV00001B/40/P

9 781456 068356